Exactly As I Am

Exactly As I Am

....

Celebrated Women Share Candid Advice

with Today's Girls on What It Takes to

Believe in Yourself

Shaun Robinson

BALLANTINE BOOKS NEW YORK

Published in the United States by Ballantine Books, an imprint of The Random House Publishing Group, a division of Random House, Inc., New York.

BALLANTINE and colophon are registered trademarks of Random House, Inc.

Library of Congress Cataloging-in-Publication Data
Robinson, Shaun.
Exactly as I am: celebrated women share candid advice with today's girls on what it takes to believe in yourself / Shaun Robinson.
p. cm.
ISBN 978-0-345-51195-9
1. Self esteem in women. 2. Self esteem in adolescence. 3. Self-confidence. 4. Celebrities—Psychology. 5. Young women—Psychology. I. Title.
BF697.5.S46R634 2009
155.3'33—dc22 2009001278

Printed in the United States of America on acid-free paper

www.ballantinebooks.com

2 4 6 8 9 7 5 3

First Edition

Design by Debbie Glasserman

*This book is dedicated to all of the girls out there—
big and small—who have ever looked in the mirror
and thought, if that image were smaller, lighter, thinner,
bigger, straighter, taller, smarter, cooler—life would be oh,
so much better. May the next glance you take make you
feel beautiful and loved exactly as you are.*

Contents

Contents

Acknowledgments

Throughout this journey, I have been extremely blessed to have had so many people help me realize this dream.

The two people who always told me I was perfect exactly as I am—Joanne and Wylie, aka, Mom and Dad. You mean the world to me. You lift me up and carry me on the wings of your love. What a lucky girl I am! I would have handpicked you myself, but God did it for me. Now, *this* calls for a Coney Island breakfast!

My angels—Grandma Curry, Mama Ashie, Grandpa Robinson, Daddy Jimmy, Mama Nony, Papa, Grandma Ruth, Jacob, and Gloria. I see you in every rainbow, in every ray of sunlight, and in every twinkle of every star. I feel you in every warm breeze, every drop of rain, and every snowflake that touches my eyelids. You live in every beat of my heart.

My entire family—I send you love from across the miles.

All of the celebrated women who took time out of their very busy schedules to help girls honor their true selves— I thank you.

Ms. Winfrey—I am eternally grateful.

Marnie Cochran, when I first met you I knew that you were "the one." Thank you for your incredible energy and guidance. I owe so much to you. And to Brian McLendon, Kim Hovey, Christine Cabello, and the entire publicity and marketing teams at Ballantine, much gratitude for continuing to be champions of this book and making it such a success!

Debra Goldstein, thank you for believing in this book and for working tirelessly to make sure my vision came to life. I know I can always count on you to be there for me.

Billie Fitzpatrick, you are an amazingly gifted woman with the most gentle voice. Thank you for creating a beautiful partnership and for helping me present our message to girls so eloquently.

Peter Harper, you really got the ball rolling for me when this project was in its infancy. Thank you for your advice and for guiding me in the right direction.

Ken Lindner—from Miami to L.A., you've been my champion for so many years. We've done some great work together!

Angela Cochran, thank you for all of your input and research, and helping me find so many of the wonderful women for this book.

Adam Jordan, I have so much appreciation for your

wonderful gift to my favorite organization, Girls Inc., and also for the use of your Rolodex.

Patrik Henry Bass, you make me laugh so much. Thank you for being such a wonderful source of information and joviality.

Lolita Files, Sherri Evans-Harris, Will Thomas, Rob Silverstein, Jeneine Doucette, Nancy Harrison, Chris Fahey, Joe Schlosser, Mandy Ellis, Alison Lee, Brenda Buchanan, Brenda Davenport, Ralph Oshiro, and Steve Chan Chee—a special thank-you for all the support you have given me throughout this project.

To all of the girls who trusted me enough to bare their souls—Jewel, Angelica, Lyric, Dasia, Alana, Ali, Bryanna, Cameron, Jacklyn, Katy, Lauren, Shayne, Tiffany, Mary, Kaylin, LaTece, Shamika, Alexandria, Ariana, Jessica, Makeda, Patrice, Pilar, Pleh, Shani, Rashri, Xiomara, Aryn, Adrienne, Aundrea, Charmaine, Marquesha, Tiesha, Kenya. Your voices give this book its heart.

Finally, this book would not have been possible without the help of the publicists, agents, and managers who represented the wonderful women I interviewed for this project. Thanks to all of you for believing in my message: Kelly Bush, Lisa Halliday, Angela DePaul, Michelle McIntyre, Megan Kopf, Lauren Kapp, Kimberly Connors, Paul Bloch, Stan Rosenfield, Brad Cafarelli, Stephen Huvane, Paul Freundlich, Heidi Schaeffer, Thea Ellis, Laura M. Wright, Kelli Haylard, Sarah Fuller, Jenn Sousa, Roger Widynowski, Kim Jakwerth, Rene Angelil, David Naranjo, Frank Amadeo, Barry Dale Johnson, Alexis Rodriguez, Matthew Trachtenberg, Patti Webster, Jamie Mendoza, Jessica Davenport, Sally Zumalt, Maurice Luque, Amanda Silverman, LB, Michelle Elisabeth, Scott Cooke, Neal

Schiff, Sahar Sanjar, Jon Leshay, Amy Pfister, Reen Nalli, Tracey Miller, Val Ackerman, Caroline Williams, Lewis Kay, Nicki Fioravante, Brendan Daly, Paula Madison, Danica Smith, Angelica Cob-Baehler, Toni DiMartino, Nicole Corcoran, Evan Morgenstein, Natalie Godwin, Karla Coleman, Tony Velasquez.

Introduction

I believe we all struggle with self-esteem, whether we are fourteen, thirty-four, or fifty-four. When we look in the mirror, enter a classroom, walk into a party, or stand up in front of a crowd to give a presentation—or, in my case, interview a celebrity live on national TV—it is completely natural to question our power, our attractiveness, and our abilities to one degree or another.

I remember feeling this way when I first auditioned for my job at *Access Hollywood*. I had come from a strong news background, having worked in several local markets. I was an award-winning journalist who had covered every news story imaginable. I was very solid "live," after anchoring countless hours of breaking news. So when I auditioned, I knew I had the credentials, but something happened when I actually got on the set of this national show that I had watched for years. Suddenly I felt terrified! When it came to reading the copy, I froze. Thoughts started swirling around in my mind: *Why me? How could they pick me? I'm sure there are many talented people trying out for this job.* The director was waiting. *Read the copy, Shaun,* I kept saying to myself. Those seconds seemed to last forever.

Somehow, I got the words out.

As soon as I got on the plane heading back to Miami, my eyes started welling up with tears. I was convinced that I had just blown a huge opportunity. How could I go from being a local news reporter to my dream job on a national entertainment show? All those negative voices of self-doubt started quickly creeping in. Then, a week later, *Access* called and told me I got the job. Wow. I couldn't believe all the time I'd wasted beating myself up! This year, I celebrate my tenth year with the show. Whenever I start to question myself and my abilities, I try to remember that time in my life.

As an entertainment reporter, I live and work in a world of celebrity, and I love covering Hollywood. It's a lot of fun meeting and getting to know the personalities who star in your favorite TV show, who you cheered for in that Oscar-winning movie, or whose music you jam to on your iPod. There are many celebrities I have become friends with because I like the people they are off-camera—genuine, down-to-earth, caring individuals. And yes, it is interesting to peek into the lives of the rich and famous, see how they spend their time, and scoop up some of their top-secret beauty and fitness tips. But as we well know, this fun pastime of celeb patrol has ballooned into a cultural obsession—and it's having a dramatic effect on young women, most notably on their self-esteem.

Over the years, including the time I've been at *Access Hollywood*, countless girls and young women have asked me in letters and emails about the stars I've met. Of varying ages, these girls want to know, "Does So-and-So really look like that in person?" "How can I be as thin as her?" "Are those stars as perfect as they look on TV?" As our entire culture has become markedly more obsessed with celebrity, the number and urgency of the inquiries from girls has increased. And more often than not, they equate the images of the stars with perfection and use what they think they're seeing—be it looks, talent, popularity, or wealth—as a barometer for their own self-worth.

I don't think the media is to blame for this over-the-top interest in celebrities, but I do think there is danger in how all women, no matter their age, compare themselves with these "perfect" women. I say this because so many of the emails and letters I receive are from girls and women writing to say they feel *less than* beautiful, *less than* perfect, and *less than* acceptable—just because they don't look like these stars or live similar lifestyles. When young women internalize this message of being less than, they essentially stunt their growth and their potential, damaging or hindering their ability to achieve their dreams. And to me, that is just not okay.

Of course, the cultural obsession with celebrity is not new, but how it is impacting the way girls and women feel about themselves has become a passionate concern of mine—so much so that over the past few years I began organizing informal task-force groups of girls and young women from around the country to talk directly about their issues of self-esteem. I wanted to hear what they had to say about confidence, role models, their relationship with their parents, and how they get along with their friends in this fast-paced, technology-driven culture. I knew being a teenager today is different than it was in my day, but I wasn't prepared for hearing about *how* different, *how* fast, and *how* stressful this time in life can be. As our younger generation, you have a lot to say, and I quickly realized that our culture needs to start hearing it! We need to tune in to how we can use the culture of celebrity in a way that will actually nurture and help girls.

So I began to seek out celebrities and other influential women to figure out what advice they might offer young women about how to nurture confidence and self-worth, based not on looks but on tangible skills and characteristics. I wanted to know what these celebrities had to say on this topic, guessing (correctly as it turned out) that in terms of self-esteem, they had very vivid memories, interesting and sometimes painful experiences, and always lots of thoughtful, caring guidance to share with the young women out there who feel so much pressure to be "thin and pretty" and who are trying to develop their own confidence.

The responses were fascinating. They shared it all. Many confessed to feeling uncool or unpopular as a teenager (Who knew the talented Virginia Madsen suffered poignant pariah trauma?) and even not fitting in later in life (Queen Latifah had to go through her own process to reconcile not fitting the traditional picture of what Hollywood expects). Many were bravely candid about not feeling as confident as they might appear in the spotlight, and told of difficult experiences that led them to a greater sense of strength.

In all cases, these women spoke frankly about how developing and holding on to self-esteem is a lifelong process. None of them came into the world thinking they were beautiful or talented, never mind perfect; rather, they grew their confidence day by day, success by success. Sure, many of them are rich and famous and very glamorous in their own right, but you will find that this outer shell is never the building block for real self-esteem. Instead, what I have gleaned from all these stars' stories and memories is that self-esteem is what you have when everything else is stripped away and what's left is what you truly believe you are inside.

We all make assumptions about who celebrities are—that they are perfect, have no self-doubts, have experienced no pain. Immediately and universally, the celebrities I interviewed not only questioned this myth of perfection but also spoke of how important it is that we all feel valued for ourselves—regardless of our body shape, hair color, skin color, or background. What I hope will become clear to you as you read this book is that stars are most certainly human beings first.

Armed with a new understanding of how celebrities really feel about themselves, I wanted to know more. I wanted to know what other accomplished women had to say about self-esteem. I decided to also approach women who had found success in areas that are not traditionally female professions, including athletics, business, and science. I interviewed the world-famous race-car driver Danica Patrick, asking her to describe her experiences in a predominantly male world; when talking with boxer Laila Ali, I asked what in her life helped her become confident at such an early age; and when interviewing actress Lisa Rinna, I asked her why she felt it important to expand beyond her success in acting and become a businesswoman as well. What I found was that all these women were once girls who, at one time or another, were trying to fit in, discover their strengths, and conquer self-doubt in order to pursue their dreams and achieve their goals.

All in all, I interviewed dozens of women celebrities and professionals. When I blended these voices with those of the young women from my task-force groups, together they created a kind of dialogue between the young women and girls of today and those women who have more or less navigated this rite of passage—a dialogue that I felt I needed to share with you.

Why This Book?

Two other events occurred in my life that made me realize this book needed to be written. The first stemmed from my personal involvement over the past few years with Girls Inc., a nonprofit organization dedicated to inspiring all girls to be "strong, smart, and bold." With roots dating to 1864, Girls Inc. has provided vital educational programs to millions of American girls, particularly those in high-risk, underserved areas. Today innovative programs help girls confront subtle societal messages about their value and potential and prepare them to lead successful, independent, and fulfilling lives. My work with Girls Inc. has not only given me access to "real girls" being affected by self-esteem issues, but it has further enabled me to talk and listen to girls of all ages and of all backgrounds who are struggling to grow up in a culture that, for all its advancements, still puts tremendous pressure on us to be pretty, thin, and nice—often at the expense of developing our brains, self-confidence, and self-esteem.

In fact, Girls Inc. recently completed a study entitled "The Supergirl Dilemma,"* which found some startling statistics, many of which might ring true for you. In a study of more than one thousand girls of various socioeconomic, racial, and ethnic backgrounds, it was shown that

- 69 percent report being concerned about their appearance;
- 52 percent worry about their weight;
- 36 percent believe that they are not supposed to be strong and tough;
- 26 percent of high school girls worry about being pressured to have sex;
- 84 percent believe they are supposed to be kind and caring;
- 55 percent believe that girls are expected to speak softly and not cause trouble;
- 44 percent believe that the smartest girls in school are not popular;
- 12 percent report that they do not know three adults to whom they could turn if they had a problem.

When I read this report, something was triggered in me: We've come so far, but we seem to have so much farther

---

*"The Supergirl Dilemma: Girls Grapple with Mounting Pressure of Expectations," a nationwide survey of school-age children conducted for Girls Inc. by Harris Interactive, 2006.

to go in terms of helping young girls become "strong, smart, and bold" women. Why is it that today with girls and women breaking all sorts of professional barriers, so many of them say they don't like themselves or wish they looked different or feel that they are somehow falling short of some sort of mark?

When I talked to the young women from across the country, they wanted to know how to feel better about themselves, so that they could make their dreams real. Above all, though, they wanted to know if other girls were thinking and feeling the same things they were. They wanted to feel *normal*. It turns out that they are all perfectly normal! Self-doubt is normal. Insecurity is normal. All the things that girls privately worry about are actually far more common than one might think.

And that's what I want to speak to. I want all of you to hear different voices—strong, supportive, loving, encouraging voices—so that you can know that you're not alone. I want you to know that there are ways you can actually build your self-esteem so that you can make your dreams come true and look toward a future bright with possibility.

A Visit with Oprah

A second event occurred that made me believe even more in the urgency and inevitability of this project. In 2007 I was invited to cover the opening of Oprah Winfrey's Leadership Academy for Girls in Johannesburg, South Africa. This trip was a tremendously moving experience for me because I witnessed girls who have nothing—many living in one-room tin shacks, without running water or electricity, who are in real and everyday danger of being raped on the way to school, whose parents rely on them to take care of younger siblings. In the face of all these obstacles, these young women were still striving to be the best they could be. And I thought to myself: *Anything is possible.* If these young women can internalize confidence, perseverance, and a sense of responsibility for themselves and others—the foundations of self-esteem—then anyone can. Indeed, when I shared the mission of my book with Oprah Winfrey, a woman I consider an inspiration and a mentor, she kindly accepted a request to share her thoughts about self-esteem for this book.

Many of us have seen footage about Oprah's school for girls, but actually being there, meeting these young girls in person and listening to them share details about their lives, brought me a new appreciation for just how special they are. It also renewed in me a desire to make this book project real. I knew it could be useful and I needed to get started.

This Book Is for You

Though every one of us, regardless of our age, can benefit from the sage advice and vivid testimonials this book offers, *Exactly As I Am* is really for those of you who are girls and young women. The road might be harder for some of you than others, you might need more help along the way, but you can still develop the inner resources to accept yourself, value yourself, and believe in yourself, which is what it all comes down to. Without self-esteem, you spend your life looking over your shoulder or in the mirror—always comparing yourself with others, always feeling like you fall short, that you are not good enough, pretty enough, thin enough—wasting precious energy that you could be directing to dreaming dreams and fulfilling goals! Self-esteem is your ticket to freedom and making your dreams come true.

The goal of this book is to inspire you to seize every opportunity to grow confidence, to know how to be comfortable in your own skin, and to accept yourself, exactly as you are. In these pages you will find all sorts of women, from all sorts of backgrounds, of varying age, race, and ethnicity, speaking about what self-esteem means to them and how they developed it. The dictionary says *self-esteem* is "confidence in one's own worth or abilities; self-respect." But we use this phrase often and loosely to mean many things. What does it mean to you? I want you to find how you can be "strong, smart, and bold," as the motto of Girls Inc. states. I want you to find how to nurture your dreams and begin to achieve some of your goals. I want you to find solace in the stories of others who have had experiences similar to yours. I want you to find a way to increase your confidence so that you can look ahead at your life with a can-do attitude and never again let doubt, fear, or insecurity stand in the way of you becoming a star in your own right—*exactly as you are.*

SHAUN ROBINSON
Los Angeles, California
October 2008

Exactly As I Am

Chapter One

You Are Who You Are

BEAUTY AND SELF-ACCEPTANCE

*It is hard to let your personality flourish when you are
pointlessly paralyzed by insecurities about your physique.
Both boys and girls can be horribly cruel and childishly
thoughtless. Character and personality are much more
important and ultimately win out. For time passes and
youthful beauty with it.* —HELEN MIRREN

Pretty . . . skinny . . . perfect.

These were the words I kept hearing over and over
again as I spoke with teenage girls across the country. What
did they love about themselves? What would they change?
What image were they trying to live up to? Whether they
lived on the East Coast or the West, in the Midwest or the
South, their voices seemed to speak in unison: "I want to be
pretty. I want to be skinny. I want perfection like I see on
TV and in the magazines." These girls created a beautiful
rainbow of skin tones, hair textures, and figures, from cur-
vaceous to boyish. They were tall like basketball players,
small like gymnasts, and in between like the girl next door.
I found them all uniquely beautiful, but they all admitted to

feeling pressure to somehow look better than they did. And it was also clear that their idea of beauty was all about being pretty and thin and perfect. What an impossible standard to live up to!

Though I could fill an entire book with stories and quotes from girls who desperately wished they looked different, here are just a few of the things they told me:

You can never be skinny enough. It makes you feel like you're never perfect because you never reach your destination.

—AMANDA, FOURTEEN

I don't have enough time to tell you all the things I would change about my body. I feel I should work out more and get fit. I'm nineteen, so I'm not so young anymore. —TARA, NINETEEN

My friends who are light-skinned always get more attention than I do because my skin is very dark and I don't have straight hair. It makes me feel like I'm not worth as much as they are.

—LAILA, FIFTEEN

I asked my mom for a new pair of jeans for my birthday, but I want her to get them a size twenty-five because I'm going on this new diet I read about. —SOPHIA, SEVENTEEN

Super-skinny is in vogue. Girls get that from the media and celebrities. I would do just about anything to be just as skinny.

—LINDSEY, SIXTEEN

Boys really like long hair, and I want to get extensions because my hair is so short. My mom told me I have to wait, but some of my friends got extensions in middle school. —MARISA, FIFTEEN

This pressure to be and feel beautiful is not new. I am sure all of you reading now have experienced it—that sense of looking in the mirror and wishing you looked different, a bit better, thinner, more beautiful . . . something closer to perfect. But what does perfect really mean, anyway? We are all vulnerable to the images of beauty all around us. These images are ubiquitous and send the unfortunate message that in order to be considered acceptable, we have to look a certain way—almost always some other way than we actually do.

Girls Inc. Link: We All Feel It

Everyone else secretly feels it, too. If you're among the young women who feel anxious about your weight or appearance as it compares with the "ideal," you're not alone. According to the Girls Inc. "Supergirl Dilemma" study*:

- 69 percent of girls interviewed are concerned about their appearance;
- 55 percent of girls actively worry about how they look;
- 34 percent believe they are too fat.

Stars in Our Eyes

Most of the girls I talked to were crystal clear on the role celebrities play in reinforcing these ideals and the so-called myth of perfection. As seventeen-year-old Carrie from New York told me, "I think there are a lot of girls who want

*"The Supergirl Dilemma: Girls Grapple with Mounting Pressure of Expectations."

to mimic the image of celebrities. They want to change themselves—they don't want to be their own person."

All around us we see celebrities with perfect hair, gleaming teeth, blemish-free, radiant skin, and of course, that perfect body. I think most people agree that it's fun to look at the beautiful photos of stars in magazines, on television, and on the Internet. But there's something wrong when we get down on ourselves for not being like those pictures. As a media insider, I can tell you that a lot of time and expert hands often go into creating those images! Yes, these women are all beautiful in their own right exactly as they are, but what you see beaming from your television screen or magazine covers are carefully arranged images that most of these women will readily admit are something of a fantasy.

Believe me, no one knows the power and influence of the media more than I do, having spent much of my career working in front of the camera and being on television. I've also been face-to-face with the so-called "most beautiful people in the world"—the ones who are often held up as the standard of beauty. You see them grace the red carpet at the Oscars, the Golden Globes, and the Grammys. How spectacular they look! And when you find yourself standing next to Angelina Jolie, Salma Hayek, Beyoncé, or Jennifer Lopez, it can be quite intimidating.

But since it's my job to interview these stars on the red carpet, I, too, am in the spotlight all of the time, and I, too, feel the pressure to look my best. Thankfully, I also have had the benefit of working with some of the greatest makeup artists, hairstylists, and wardrobe consultants in Hollywood. When I get out of the makeup chair and put on an expensive designer gown to host the official Academy Awards pre-show, do I feel beautiful and confident? Of course. But what many viewers don't know is that it takes a *loooong* time to get ready for events like that!

It's hard to feel good about yourself when the image you see doesn't quite live up to the standards that we set for ourselves. Of course, some of the girls I spoke with were able to feel good about the way they looked despite the pressure to be pretty and thin and perfect, like the celebrities. Karen, a fifteen-year-old from Atlanta, said, "I like everything about me—my eyes, my hair, my skin. There's nothing I would change. This is how God made me, and I appreciate it."

But you can probably relate to many of the girls I talked to who admitted feeling inadequate about the way they look, tying a lot of the reason to the images of celebrities that surround them. As Katie, a fourteen-year-old girl from New York, said, "I feel like the media is controlling people's lives. Some girls look up to their favorite actress or singer who is really skinny, and they strive to be really skinny just like their idol." Sarah, a particularly eloquent fifteen-year-old from Los Angeles, hit the nail right on the head when she said, "Many girls can't even tell that the faces on magazine covers are retouched. They think that's how the model or actress actually looks. It makes you question yourself."

Behind the Glamour

So here's the real question: Does measuring up to the perceived ideal of beauty—that is, actually being pretty and thin (or even just appearing to be so)—make all those amazing and glamorous women feel better about themselves than the rest of us do? Are they happier, more secure in themselves? This is one of the things I set out to learn in interviewing the dozens of celebrities in this book. I wanted to know how and what they really think and feel, because more than anything, I believe that young women need to know and understand that these images of perfection they see are of real people, with many of the same doubts, insecurities, and questions they have.

Of course, the responses were as varied as the women themselves, but what was most fascinating to learn was that nearly all of the women struggled—either earlier in their lives or currently—with accepting themselves exactly as they are. So many of them felt ugly, embarrassed, inadequate, or awkward—not unlike regular girls today. Yes, we all have similarities when it comes to feeling like we oftentimes don't measure up!

Here is some of what they shared.

Lisa Rinna on Looking Different

Actor, dancer, singer, entrepreneur, and mother Lisa Rinna is so glamorous when you see her on the red carpet. But she can still remember the pain of being called ugly—all because she looked different from the rest of her peers.

"I know exactly what it feels like to have people dislike you and make fun of you because of the way you look. I was very dark-skinned as a child and very skinny. I was darker than the fair-haired, fair-skinned children in Medford, Oregon, in 1970. I didn't look like anyone, and I wore really short Izod dresses and I was endlessly teased, called Black Cow. It was traumatic. Before, when we lived in Newport Beach, California, I had never thought twice about how I looked. Until age seven, I felt accepted and loved for who I was and how I looked."

JANET JACKSON ON LOOKING IN THE MIRROR

It's hard to believe that the indomitable Janet Jackson, whose physique is legendary, at one time felt desperately unhappy about how she looked. She shared with me this story:

> "I had a very difficult time looking at myself in the mirror. So often I would cry because I didn't find myself talented or attractive at all. I didn't have Naomi Campbell's legs. I didn't think I was pretty. I didn't like my body. My level of confidence was very low. I struggled for years—I mean *years!*"

Janet, like so many of the girls and women I spoke with, had a keen sense of where this self-doubt began.

> "I think society plays a major part. The women we see in videos and all the stars in the magazines and models on the catwalk are portrayed as flawless. And if you don't look like that, it could make anyone feel less than."

IMAN ON FEELING INADEQUATE

Iman is among the most glamorous models in the world. At almost five feet nine, with spectacular bone structure and grace, she's simply stunning. Yet she, too, was painfully affected by the idea of "measuring up" as a young woman.

> "I struggled with self-esteem. It was quite difficult as I became a teenager, not realizing that these feelings are a rite of passage. I was extremely tall for my age and extremely skinny. My neck was extraordinarily long, and I hated looking so different

from everyone else. I used to wear collared shirts turned up to hide my neck!"

SHARON STONE ON SELF-DOUBT

....

The charismatic Sharon Stone just oozes confidence when you see her on the red carpet, but she didn't always feel so self-assured. Now she has a message for young women who are in their prime. Like so many girls, it took her a long time to see the beauty in herself.

"I didn't think I was pretty until I was thirty-three years old. Think of all the time I wasted!"

As you can see, many of these fabulous ladies questioned their self-image just as you and I have. Even though they are now famous, they, too, felt less than perfect.

Boobs, Curves, and Wanting to Look Like Someone Else

Like the celebrities quoted here, many of the girls I spoke with just wanted to look different. Not different as in exotic, but different from themselves, more like someone else. I remember vividly feeling this way when I was younger. For me, it was about my hair. I was really obsessed with having long hair. When I was really little, I used to attach scarves to my braids and move my head from side to side, swinging my long "hair." My mother even gave me one of her old synthetic ponytails to play with, and I was in heaven! Swing, swing, swing! But one day my mom actually cut her own shoulder-length, relaxed hair and started wearing it in an

Afro to teach me a lesson. As she says now, "My friends thought I was nuts, but I wanted Shaun to know there was more than one way to be beautiful." Even when I was older, I was still obsessed with my hair—Should I relax it, let it go natural? By the time I was a teenager, and like so many African American girls who wanted straight, long hair, I always made sure I went to a beauty salon every six or eight weeks to get that relaxer. Despite Mom's lesson, I still thought the prettiest girls had long, straight hair.

Many girls spoke to me about how they felt pressure to not only be pretty and thin but also sexy and curvy—talk about trying to be everything! As seventeen-year-old Bree from Los Angeles told me, "Everyone has the desire to be thin, but you still need the big butt, and the big boobs."

Seventeen-year-old Michelle from New York told me that "most girls wish they had bigger butts, bigger chests, different face structure, and better clothing." Sound familiar? How can you expect yourself to be both curvy and bony? Impossible!

Another disheartening thing I heard from the African American girls I talked to was that skin color—light versus dark—was still as significant an issue today as it was when I was growing up. As eighteen-year-old Paula shared, "I've learned [to be] comfortable with myself. I've accepted that I am a different black girl, and that's fine. But it's hard when you live in a society where they don't promote your beauty. I see magazines, but I don't see dark-skinned African Americans."

And fourteen-year-old Katie pointed out with the clear vision of a much older girl, "You would never see a music video with the main girl in the video who the guy is trying to pursue having dark skin with locks. They're always some skinny, light-skinned, straight-haired girl. They are basically sending the message that these are the kinds of girls that are pretty and if you don't look like them, then you are not as beautiful."

And eighteen-year-old Zoe pretty much summed it up: "Society makes it as if light-skinned girls are in, and [not] us dark-skinned girls. It really does hurt a lot to feel that you're ugly."

Again, these girls are feeling badly about themselves because they do not measure up to some myth of perfection. As Zoe told me, girls hear that inner voice saying, *"God, I wish I was light-skinned, I wish I had a fat butt, I wish my body wasn't so small, I wish my hair wasn't this short, I wish* . . . It is just so much I wish, I wish, I wish."

So what do you do with this pressure?

Jennifer Love Hewitt on Empowering Yourself

Actress Jennifer Love Hewitt spent most of her teen years on television. Growing up in an industry that puts so much pressure on girls to act a certain way wasn't easy, but she thanks her mom for helping her believe in herself no matter what. She told me:

> "My mom taught me the things that make you beautiful and the things that make you *you*. If you are not as skinny as everyone else, but you're happy, then be happy! It's okay not to be the skinniest person at school. Don't let other people tell you how beautiful you are; tell yourself how beautiful you are. If you tell yourself that you're not worth very much and not as beautiful as everybody else, not as smart or not as skinny or not as 'whatever,' then pretty soon your body chemistry starts to believe that. The only person who is

creating those really 'bummed-out' feelings and who doesn't really feel good about themselves is you.

"But if you wake up and you put on an outfit that makes you feel good, it doesn't matter if you're the tallest, shortest, skinniest, or biggest, or you have braces or curly hair or straight hair or whatever it is, you walk down that hallway every single day and walk down that red carpet and you feel good about who you are. If you tell yourself before you leave your house, 'You know what, I'm a really cool person, and people would be lucky to get to know me because I have something to offer the world,' then that's what people are going to believe about you. We put too much faith in other people telling us who we are versus teaching people who we are. That has taken me a really, really long time to learn, and I'm almost thirty, and I still have not perfected it. But it really helps when you realize how much of your own power you have and can use every day."

Do We Really Need to Change?

Let's face it: It's not like tomorrow we are all going to wake up and *not* care about how we look. But what we *are* going to do together throughout this book is learn how to resist comparing ourselves with others and realize that beauty comes in all colors, shapes, and textures.

Things change. We change.

Liking yourself exactly the way you are doesn't mean you don't wear makeup, color your hair, or wear extensions. It doesn't mean that you can't have a desire to shave off a few pounds. But to me there is a big difference between wanting to change or augment a few features and obsessing about how you look or going to great lengths to alter your appearance. It seems to me that when we compare ourselves with other females in ways that are unhealthy, we really begin to sell ourselves short. I know. Trust me, I'm not immune! Like so many young women, I used to want larger breasts. There were many times that I wanted them bigger just so I could fill out my tops. I used to frequent this one very popular women's clothing store because the clothes fit me so nicely. Years later, I noticed that many of their extra-small tops were too big and I asked the salesgirl why there seemed to be something different about the cut because I knew I had not lost weight. She said that because so many of their customers had had boob jobs, they started altering the measurements of their clothes to accommodate the larger breasts!

It's taken me some years and life experience, but I've come to really appreciate my body type. I love my small breasts, and if I want to fill out a top or designer gown, girlfriend, there are so many ways to do that—with one of the many new bras on the market or the very popular "chicken cutlets"! I have friends who have had boob jobs. These are confident, secure women, but trust me, they were that way *before* they got their breasts enlarged. Their confidence didn't balloon as their chests got larger, and they certainly didn't have the surgery to look like or please anyone else. And more important, they made this decision when they were adults and after tons of research on the dangers and risks (because there are many) of breast implants.

My experience is very similar to what a number of the young women in the task-force groups told me. So many of them talked about how hard it is not to get obsessed with the way you look, especially when it comes to body image. You might even know some girls who might be getting plastic surgery for their sixteenth birthday! Clearly, you are all under the same pressure to look good. That's why we're busting (pardon the pun) this all out in the open! And when I talked to the celebrities, they all said the same thing— they, too, feel pressure to look a certain way, especially under the intense media spotlight. But, even though their business puts so much pressure on them to look good, they wisely pointed out that beauty is, indeed, only skin-deep.

Helen Mirren on Taking the Long View

This Academy Award–winning British actress, whose straight-talking elegance shines through especially now that she is in her sixties, is quite clear about what she can change and what she won't. As she shared with me:

> "I am not and never have been what you might call 'beautiful.' I am not being self-deprecating, but I do know what real beauty is and I never had it. Lucky me! Neither did I have a remotely 'fashionable' look, for obviously, looks change in fashion as much as clothes. . . . In the late sixties, when Twiggy was the only way to look, I had a classic hourglass figure and legs to match—still have!"

Helen was fortunate enough to have a strong familial support system to pull her through her own doubts (we'll talk more about the role of parents and other support a little later in this book). As she pointed out to me, "I had the advantage of parents who, while not being blindly and ridiculously flattering, were supportive and sensitive to what young girls go through. They made us feel proud of simply what we were, whether it fit into the fashion or not."

Helen has the wisdom of the long view.

"What actually happens is that you grow up and everything gets better. You don't miraculously turn into the naturally thin Kate Moss, especially if your method to do so is anorexia (that way, only a horrible sickness and a hideous body follow). You grow to understand that no, you will never look or live like they do in magazines, but your world is better and bigger because hopefully it has love and fun in it. If it does not have love and fun in it, then make it do so as soon as possible!

"You must start by loving yourself. Also, remember, life is a lot longer than twenty-five years, and it can get better and better if you have not invested it all in your looks. If you have, beware: danger ahead!"

Garcelle Beauvais-Nilon on Telling Girls They're Pretty

My friend Garcelle Beauvais-Nilon knows how much pressure girls are under to be pretty. The actress and former model says adults, sometimes unintentionally, feed into that.

"We need to stop telling little girls that they're really pretty and instead say, 'Wow, you're really smart!' or 'You're really good at that!' I think if we start emphasizing other aspects early on, instead of stressing the superficial right away, girls will think of themselves differently."

Kelly Clarkson on Embracing the Imperfect

Kelly Clarkson, who skyrocketed to fame after winning *American Idol* and has since become a beloved international pop star with eight singles on the

Billboard Hot 100 chart, has a frank, call-it-like-it-is approach to herself and others. "In real life, I don't look like the way I do in videos," she admitted.

"It's all lighting—you have a team of people making you look your best. If everyone had a team of people making them look their best, then maybe people wouldn't be so down on themselves. The flaws and the vulnerability are what make people attractive. The imperfect almost makes it perfect.

"Honestly, everyone is different. That's what makes us all cool. I'm not the hottest pop star, or the ugliest. At the end of the day, it's hard for everyone. . . . I don't understand why everyone would want to be like somebody else. And it's really hard to describe because at the end of the day, there is always going to be someone smarter, prettier, and more talented. You're never going to be that top person, so why even care about it?"

GABRIELLE UNION ON CHASING THE IDEAL

The talented and tenacious actress and former model Gabrielle Union, another friend of mine, was very honest with me when she talked about learning to accept yourself instead of always trying to be something you're not:

"The reality is there is always going to be something that makes you second-guess yourself. The goal should be trying to feel comfortable in your own skin. . . . When I finally jumped off the carousel of chasing the ideal, it was like a monkey hopped off my back."

Self-esteem. I hear all these celebrities saying the same thing about one of the ways it begins: accepting and realizing that your beauty is not about your face or your body;

it's about what's inside of you and what you choose to do with your time, energy, and, ultimately, your life. If you can try to think a little more about what's important to you on the inside, instead of focusing so much on how you look on the outside, you might just find yourself in a stronger place—a place in which you can resist comparing yourself with others, a place where you can celebrate your differences, a place that will sustain you for life. I don't think this problem will go away, but what we can do is become more aware of the fact that beauty is not just one thing. We are all beautiful in our own, singular way.

INDIA.ARIE ON SELF-ACCEPTANCE

India.Arie is one of my favorite singers. I love her individuality, the positive messages in her music, and her quiet confidence. She told me something that I think all girls, all women, who at times may feel less than, should remember:

"I am on this journey to learn where I fit in this world, and to define myself and to love myself. Just like a lot of people reading this book, I flip through any magazine and realize very clearly that there are not many people in the music industry who look the way I do . . . my nose and teeth and hair—all of it. I'm not the popular look and I am constantly reminded of that. But rather than looking at that and saying I have no place, I make my own place. I hold a place. I hold a space in the music industry that is to speak for the girl who feels like an outcast, the person who is unapologetically different. The woman who says, 'My money maker is not my body, it's my mind' . . . the everyday woman."

Oprah Winfrey on Seeing Yourself Differently

All the girls, the celebrities, and the professional women I talked to seemed to arrive at the same conclusion: You've got to become comfortable in your own skin. That doesn't mean you shouldn't stop trying to be your best, to look good, and to make reasonable changes that make you feel good, but it does mean cherishing yourself, perfect or not. And quite often it means finally learning to see yourself through new eyes. Take, for example, the experience of Ms. Oprah Winfrey.

Oprah helped more than a hundred South African girls who came from dire poverty see themselves through new eyes when she opened her Leadership Academy in Johannesburg. She herself knows how nurturing a girl and feeding her positive messages from early on can make such a difference in her life. When she was a child, the kind words of a woman she hardly knew touched her heart forever.

"When I was eight years old I met a woman, Tish Hooker, who uttered one sentence to me that I never forgot. She said, 'You are as pretty as a speckled pup, and you have such beautiful bee-stung lips.' I didn't know what a speckled pup was or what bee-stung lips meant, but I remember going home after church and staring at myself in the mirror because a pretty lady had said to me that I was pretty. That special moment stayed with me all my life because her simple words—said with sincerity, graciousness, and kindness—made me begin to see myself differently."

Alicia Keys on Defining Ourselves Differently

Grammy-winning singer Alicia Keys's album *As I Am* will always be one of my favorites. She sings about loving yourself just because God created you in his eyes. She wanted me to share this with you:

"There are so many incredible and strong women, but I think the majority of the images that we see on TV, magazines, movies, videos, et cetera, make us feel less than perfect. In many ways, there are so many unrealistic images that are shown to define beauty and they are impossible to live up to. I think they affect us and make us question ourselves. We need more variety in how we depict beauty and define intelligence—there's so much more than what is often featured."

Pretty . . . skinny . . . perfect.
   Swing, swing, swing.
   I want, I wish, if only . . .
   There is no ideal beauty, no matter what we see as we click through the channels on the television, or turn the pages in the magazines—and certainly no matter what we hear from the boys in school. There is no one shape, size, hair texture, or skin or eye color that is more beautiful than the rest. If you allow someone else to define your beauty, you will never feel that you measure up, because perfection does not exist. Your self-esteem will grow when you stop wasting time wishing you looked like "her" and begin owning and embracing and loving every curve, color, and curl on your body! When you are comfortable with who you are, you are naturally more confident, and a confident girl is the most attractive one in the room. The journey to self-acceptance doesn't happen overnight. It's like going on vacation: It's often a long trip, but once you arrive, you get to take your shoes off and enjoy the view!

Chapter Two

· · · · · · · · ·

You Are Worth It

GROW CONFIDENCE

Not everybody is a rose. You can be a tulip, a daffodil, anything you want to be. In order to develop confidence, you don't have to aspire to be on the poster down the street. There is a place for you—a wonderful, gorgeous place for you. —SHARON STONE

Confidence. It's a cornerstone of self-esteem, that's for sure, though I think we can all admit that it isn't always so easy to come by. I know for myself, when I feel in command of what I'm doing—when I really feel strong and capable— those are the times I feel the best about myself. And the times that I give in to that nasty little voice of doubt about what I can do or be, well, those are just some of the most trying days, I'll tell you!

The girls I talked with in my task-force groups had a lot to say about self-doubt: where it comes from (criticism, fear), how it affects us (keeping us from really going for our dreams, which is of course unacceptable!), and the fact that nearly everyone, at one time or another, grapples with a lack of confidence. Danielle, a petite sixteen-year-old from the West Coast, nailed it when she said, "I don't believe that girls who act so confident are always confident. Every single person has insecurities, because naturally, we're only human."

Others had a variety of honest comments to add:

Unfortunately, I doubt myself on a regular basis—about sixty to seventy percent of the time. —NICOLE, SIXTEEN

I feel doubtful about one third of the time, but then I quickly reassure myself that I can do whatever I put my mind to; determination is all I need to succeed. —BECCA, SEVENTEEN

To be honest, I doubt myself occasionally, but who doesn't? I know that I shouldn't, but even though my grades are good, I always feel there is room for improvement. —ROBIN, EIGHTEEN

Sometimes the pressure of school makes me feel insecure because I am surrounded by amazing girls who succeed at academics, arts, and athletics. —LOUISA, FIFTEEN

That's what this chapter is about: sharing the ups and downs, the highs and the lows, of girls and famous women alike, so we can start to see the bigger picture of where true confidence comes from, and how we can grow it within ourselves.

Family as Foundation

Can you grow confidence? Absolutely. How? Now, *that* is an excellent question! Does it come from believing in ourselves, from hard work, from learning how to pick ourselves up when we fall? Yes, yes, and yes.

It also comes from having the support of your family. Some of the girls in the task-force groups told me that the love and nurturing they receive from their parents is the single most important factor in their self-esteem. Others, especially those who do not have encouraging or supportive parents, found role models outside of the home who have helped to inspire and buoy them.

Listening to these very thoughtful, ambitious young women from across the country, I made an observation: It seemed to me that those who had the most solid relationships with their parents were those who seemed most sure of themselves. Zoe, eighteen years old, from New York City, said, "Since I was little, my mom always signed me up for girls' programs and activities. That's what helped to build my self-esteem."

Alex, seventeen and also from New York, said, "My parents have always had a lot of confidence in me. They've never told me, 'You're smart and this and that,' but they always let me know that I was important."

Abby, seventeen, from Los Angeles, said, "My godmother and my aunt have helped me believe in myself. They both remind me of how smart and gifted I am. They tell me how bright my future can be."

And fifteen-year-old Louisa, also from Los Angeles, said, "Knowing that my parents love me unconditionally and are proud of me no matter what—this is what inspires me to accept my flaws and always try harder."

Some of you might relate to these girls; in fact, I bet that a majority of you do. There is no doubt in my mind that it would have been a much tougher road for me had I not had a very supportive family to encourage me along the way. My mother has always been the nurturer, the one who would hug me and tell me everything was going to be okay. My dad has always been very philosophical and practical in his advice: "Stay spiritual, stay cool, and remember, baby, a setback is a setup for a comeback!"

It really helps to have parents or other family members who love you unconditionally, but it's important to remember to actually let that love and support in! When you keep in mind how much these key players in your life believe in you and love you—and have since day one—you can carry it with you, wherever you go, like a golden locket of strength next to your heart.

Many of the celebrities and professional women and athletes also spoke of how their parents' love and belief in them helped them feel confident.

LAILA ALI ON DOING ANYTHING YOU WANT TO DO

I met boxer Laila Ali a couple of years ago. She is a woman who exudes power. As the daughter of Muhammad Ali, himself famous for both his boxing *and* his confidence, she attributes a lot of her own self-confidence and success to her parents' belief in her. As she put it: "I was brought up being taught that I can do anything I want to do. The way my parents acted and spoke to me made me turn into the person I am today." Sound familiar? Just like her dad!

Laila took this belief and nurtured a winning attitude—a mindset that she used even before she stepped into the boxing ring.

"With boxing you have to have a lot of confidence to go into the ring in the first place. I had to close my eyes and dream and feel what I could do. It made me feel good and like I accomplished something just getting in there and boxing. I always planned to be undefeated, planned to be the best, planned to be world champion. It was more a question of performing the way I intended to perform than winning."

CANDACE PARKER ON PLAYING BALL

I met L.A. Sparks basketball star and recent Olympic gold medalist Candace Parker on a flight from New York to Los Angeles. She had just made her first dunk in the WNBA, and would go on to win Olympic Gold in China a month later. I loved her confidence, and wanted to find out if this young woman had always been comfortable in her own skin. Here's what she told me when I spoke to her in between her many practices:

"I grew up with parents and brothers who were really encouraging of me starting [basketball] at a young age, and really complimentary about my playing. They basically told me that I could do anything I put my mind to. Though it's an asset now, the toughest thing for me when I was younger was my height—I was always tall—and not knowing how to carry myself because everybody was shorter than me. My family told me to keep my head high and be proud of who I am. I think that's the reason why I believe in myself, because it started in my foundation, my family.

"My parents and brothers taught me that if you don't have confidence, you're going to get halfhearted results. Even if you have to fake it; fake the confidence and you'll start believing it."

Of course, years of practice and playing helped Candace become an all-star collegiate champion as well as a starter on the United States Olympic team, but it was her belief that she *should* be proud of herself and could do anything that fueled her success. In no small part, she owed this attitude to the encouragement she received from her parents and her brothers. Her family were her role models, cementing her belief in herself and letting her grow confidence.

This was true of another amazing woman I met during my travels.

Gina Davis on Never Saying Never

It takes guts and courage for a woman to want to be an agent for the FBI, a male-dominated world if there ever was one. And that's just what Gina Davis has. This African American woman actually began her career as an accomplished economist. It was her mother's voice that made the biggest difference to her, giving her the push she needed when she felt doubtful about switching careers.

"One thing my mom always told me was 'Don't ever say you can't do anything until you try.' That applied to running around the corner or drawing a picture. My mother was adamant. If you tried it, and you couldn't do it, that's another thing. But she never wanted to hear the words 'I can't.' It just wasn't allowed. It wasn't a type of thinking that existed in our house. So when it came to switching careers, I decided to simply try to take the FBI exam. I passed. That's how it all started for me."

Jennifer Love Hewitt on Celebrating Yourself

Just like Gina Davis, it was Jennifer Love Hewitt's mother who inspired her to grow confidence.

"My mom was great for me because she taught me how to celebrate how I was different. She wanted me to celebrate what made me me. I wasn't confident at all as a teenager; sometimes I'm still not. But I try to exude confidence even when I don't feel that way. If I can summon that emotion, it can sometimes help to really feel that way."

Being Strong No Matter What

Not everyone can say that her family is really there for her. Your situation might be like some of the young ladies I spoke with who told me they did not have that nurturing environment at home.

Seventeen-year-old Rachel, from New York, was one such girl, though she seems invincible nonetheless. Listen to her story:

"I don't really have a very close relationship to my family and they don't really acknowledge the things that I do, but it doesn't make me feel worthless. There are times when I get really sad, but it doesn't make me feel like I'm not smart, or I'm not good enough at this, because I feel like all that matters is that I know what I'm accomplishing and doing. Nothing I do is good enough for my family. It's just like, I can never do enough. But it only makes me work harder."

And though Rachel doesn't think her parents are "raising her right," she thinks their mistakes have made her "a little more independent." When I asked her if she had role models outside of her family who have inspired or encouraged her, she told me about a fifth-grade teacher who was very "motherly" toward her, who at one point told her, "Rachel, you don't have to be afraid of me. I'm here to help you and guide you." That was comforting to Rachel.

Kimberly, age sixteen, said, "It hurts to know that your parents are the ones that are supposed to be there. You look at other kids and you see how supportive their families are, and it hurts a little bit. I have a very clear memory from when I was six and I was sitting in the kitchen. My mother looked at me straight in the eyes and said, 'Nobody's ever going to care about you. You have to take care of yourself.' I was traumatized after that, but I learned a very valuable lesson: You need to care about yourself."

Listening to these girls, I could see that they were tough—in body, mind, and spirit. And like all the young women I spoke to, they were realists, ready to take on the world—not with stars in their eyes but with all their heart.

Being realistic and being kind to yourself are some of the ways that the celebrities and professional achievers I talked to coped with adversity and criticism—from parents, teachers, and other people in positions of authority.

GABRIELLE UNION ON NOT FEELING GOOD ENOUGH

Gabrielle talked freely with me about feeling like she didn't measure up, a feeling that definitely took its toll on her confidence when she was growing up.

"When I was in junior high, I was not feeling good enough, smart enough, pretty enough. I'd go home after school and my parents would say, 'You have to be bigger, badder, better. Your A average is okay, but why don't you get an A plus? You got a ninety-six, but why did you miss the one question?'

"I'd score twenty points playing basketball, and my dad, who was my coach, would say, 'Well, you did miss those two free throws.' I was never good enough for anybody—not my parents, not boys, no one. To make matters worse, I was constantly surrounded by people who were achieving everything."

Sharon Stone on People Who Make
You Feel Small

Sharon Stone, the Oscar-nominated actress and human-rights activist, famous for both her candor and her confidence, shared with me a particularly poignant memory:

> "I remember struggling so hard in history. I was in the fourth or fifth grade, and I had always had straight As. Suddenly I was having a hard time. I started working harder and staying up really late and working on an extra paper and putting my all into it, thinking, *Well, maybe this will do it. Maybe if I do this extra work, maybe I will somehow catch up or get it all back together or better.* And I did this big paper, something like a twenty-page paper, and gave it to my history teacher and she threw it in the trash! She wouldn't even allow me to help myself do better. I thought that was a pretty unattractive way to treat a fourth- or fifth-grader who was killing herself to try to figure out how to do better. I think you are always going to have people who want to make you feel small, to break you, beat you down. The world is not full of people trying to make the world a better place. But the world always has *some* people who are trying to make it a better place. The important thing is that you are one of *those* people. And that when you encounter the other people, you understand that nobody is good at everything, even you."

Prudence Hostetter on Asking
"Dumb" Questions

Whenever I step onto a plane, I have a habit of peeking into the cockpit to glance at the pilot. Something makes me think I might be able to tell if they've had enough sleep or are hungover from a night out on the town, in which case I would hit the nearest exit. To my delight, a couple of years ago, I peeked inside and saw that our captain was a woman—something you don't often see. I learned that her name was Captain Prudence Hostetter. Later in the flight, I passed a note to her through the flight attendant, saying I wanted to interview her. She agreed, mainly because she had a lot to share about confidence and how to build it up in yourself. Captain Hostetter recalls an experience early in her life that definitely impacted her confidence.

"I always remember my second-grade teacher writing my parents a note on my report card that said, 'Prudence often has her hand up to answer *but* invariably has the wrong answer.' After my parents read that to me, I never raised my hand again in any class! Which is sad because I probably missed out on a lot of information always believing that the rest of the class knew it all.

"There are no dumb questions—even if a question has been asked before, ask it anyway. It's your turn to learn. Explore and love life. I have always appreciated the saying 'Dance as if no one is watching, live like there is no tomorrow, and love as if your life depends upon it.'

She might have been silenced temporarily, but clearly Captain Hostetter did not let that one teacher stop her from believing in herself!

Gloria Estefan on Silencing the Critics

In addition to winning multiple Grammy Awards, Gloria Estefan is a mother and a children's book author, among many other things. When I interviewed her on the *Access Hollywood* set about self-esteem, she encouraged girls to not listen to those negative, critical voices—whether they are teachers, parents, friends, or frenemies.

"There is always going to be somebody who's negative. Don't listen to the negativity. The energy that you put out into the world is the energy that you are going to receive back. And if you are really positive about what you want to do and you are full of energy and you persevere and you work hard, then you will get to your goal. Slowly but surely, pick little goals and try to get to that little goal. You need to give yourself immediate success and feedback. Whatever you want to change in your life, you can do it, it just takes a plan and it takes persevering and working very hard toward it."

Don't Let Anything Block Your Path

In the past, if I got a test back and I did not meet my expectations, I would get upset and start to put myself down. Then I would start to look at all of my other work and realize I am capable of doing good work and I cannot let one assignment block my path to success. —Becca, seventeen

If You Fall, Get Back Up

Nurturing confidence means not freaking out when something goes wrong, when people reject or criticize you. When you get to the other side of the experience, you'll understand that you *can* weather most storms, and that if your roots are strong, your foundation solid, any kind of setback will only make you stronger.

Confidence doesn't simply appear out of thin air. Sometimes it comes from other people believing in you; sometimes you have to earn it; and sometimes it comes from facing your fears and overcoming obstacles. For me, confidence is an intangible thing that begins inside, a belief in myself that has enabled me to try to do different things in my life, even if I encounter some roadblocks along the way.

When I was a young reporter just starting out, one of my first jobs was at a television station in Michigan. I really loved going out in the field, meeting people, and gathering stories, and I received many compliments from viewers, but it seemed as though my news director was always criticizing my work. I was rarely given positive feedback—just a lot of nitpicking. I finally realized that I wasn't going to get the guidance and support that I needed from that news director, so I started looking for another job. Good thing, because a few weeks later, the news director pulled me aside and said he didn't think I had what it took to make it in the television business. I simply responded by telling him that I had (just) found another job in a bigger television market! He was stunned. Even if he didn't think so, *I* knew that I could be successful. Hard work and a belief in yourself pays off.

MEREDITH VIEIRA ON HAVING WHAT IT TAKES

When I think of role models in my life, I certainly think of Meredith Vieira. The veteran journalist and *Today* show co-host has racked up multiple Emmy Awards throughout her career. She's learned a lot about tenacity in the very tough field of broadcasting, and the road was sometimes a challenging one for her as a young reporter. This is the advice she has for all of you who are just starting out on the journey of building confidence and figuring out your direction in life:

> "Let me tell you what my father said to me the day I was fired from my first job in television. My boss told me that I didn't have

what it takes. When my dad found me crying on my bed, he asked me, 'Do you believe you have what it takes?' I said, 'Yes,' to which he replied, 'Then why do you care what anyone else thinks? There will be naysayers all through life, so you have to believe in yourself.'

"For the record, I went back to my boss and confronted him. I told him that no matter what he thought, I was definitely going to make it. And you know what? He hired me back on the spot."

All of us encounter criticism and naysayers, people who question our abilities. But you have to listen to your inner voice—even when it's saying different things from the voices around you. Some of you ladies might start out with stronger roots, but all of you can grow that belief in yourself.

> *I feel most confident when the odds are against me and everyone thinks I will say the wrong answer; it's then I perform beyond what they ever imagined.* —Abby, seventeen

Sharon Stone on Being Knocked Down

When I talked to Sharon Stone about this subject, she said:

"I think confidence comes from having been knocked down and having gotten back up. I love that song 'That's Life' by James Brown. It's the one that really rocks for me. I remember when it was hard for me to do the first *Basic Instinct* and to play that part. Oh, I got so much resistance and I was getting kicked around. I would just go to my trailer, lie on the floor, put on James Brown's 'That's Life' till the windows rattled, then quietly go back to the set and wait until they said, 'Action.'"

Patti LaBelle on Looking Within for Strength

Grammy Award–winning singer Patti LaBelle is truly one of my favorite people on this planet. I love her dearly and was so happy when she shared some of her advice with me for this book. Having lived an amazing life of both triumphs and trials, Ms. LaBelle captured the essence of this aspect of confidence when she told me:

"You have to pick yourself up and look into yourself. If something is not working in your life and you feel like your confidence is slipping, it's not always your mother or father's fault; it's not always because your best friend hurt you or what's going on in your life; sometimes it's just you. Sometimes we don't want to take the blame for it. I've become this woman at sixty-three, and now things are being given to me—opportunities and record deals and parts in movies and things like that. I think it's because people are now seeing such a positive, kick-butt person, which I wasn't before and which I wasn't not so many years ago. I grew into this woman I am today."

Candace Parker on Being Hurt

WNBA star Candace Parker's experience with injuries hits on the same themes:

"I got hurt [playing basketball] at the University of Tennessee, and I had to have reconstructive surgery in my knee. I remember waking up and the doctors said I was going to be out for a year and then I'd need another surgery. I looked at my dad, who has always been my rock through tough times and always believed in me. I just started crying. Then he said, 'I'm going to give you this minute, this second, this hour, to cry, then your full motivation should be to recover from this. Then there will be no more tears, no more sadness. You turn those tears into sweat.' And that's what I did. I haven't looked back since. I'm really lucky to have him to push me because I don't know what I would have done. That's the time a lot of people would have crumbled and never recovered from it, but put your mind to it, work out, work hard."

Candace Parker was clearly able to face her biggest fear—injury—and triumph over it. What is your biggest fear? Maybe you're afraid to stand out from the crowd? Maybe you're frightened of calling attention to yourself? What would be required for you to stare those fears down?

JENNIFER HUDSON ON STAGE FRIGHT

When Jennifer Hudson sings, she is fearless. With a voice like that, who wouldn't be? But when the Academy Award–winning actress and I spoke about confidence, she told me how she had to conquer the demon of self-doubt:

> "Back in school I used to get stage fright. In order to get past it, I would remind myself that we all are the same on the inside. We all have the same fears and insecurities. Everyone goes through the same emotions. The difference with me is that I have learned to face my fear. Girls who want to get somewhere in their lives have to learn to face fear."

The simplicity of that idea—that we are all the same on the inside—has tremendous power to put fears in perspective and keep them at bay *while* we work on our confidence. As Jennifer reminds us:

"I've always been comfortable enough to live in my own world. I think that is part of what helped me build my confidence. I can't tell you how many times I started to feel insecure, but then I would stop and remind myself about the standards I wanted to live up to. Then all of a sudden, it doesn't matter what anyone has to say."

Sometimes fearing change can get in our way. Years ago, I experienced one of the most trying times of my life. Not long after I had gotten married, left a good job, and moved to a new city, my marriage fell apart. Around the same time, my stepfather, to whom I was very close, passed away after a long illness. Not only that, but one of my closest friends—a girl I talked to almost every day—died suddenly at a young age. It seemed like my entire world was coming apart. Eventually, I found myself moving back home with my mom, without a job, sleeping in my old room, not knowing where the next step would take me or even *how* to take the next step. For me, it was the love and support of my mother and father that helped get me through. They both just kept saying that this dark period would pass and everything would be okay. They knew I would get back on track, I just had to *believe* that I would. After a period of intense grief over the loss of two people very close to me and regular pity parties about not having a job, I found my footing once again. My parents were there to support me, but they couldn't do it *for* me. I had to find it within myself to get up, dust myself off, and face the world again. If you can find the power within, you have discovered one of the tools for growing confidence.

When I look at my life now and how blessed I am with such a wonderful career and amazing family, I realize how much time I wasted doubting myself and my ability to turn things around.

It's very difficult to stay focused and believe in ourselves when we are dealing with intense emotions like fear or disappointment or loss. And it's hard for these feelings not to leak into other areas of our lives. But if we surround ourselves with people who believe in us (as I did with my family and good friends), we eventually come through the other side.

Reality Bites

In Atlanta, sixteen-year old Tamara voiced a common sentiment: "If you put your mind to it, you can do it," she said. Another thing I heard frequently was put especially well by Nicole, age sixteen: "I believe that I can succeed, but there is always an inner feeling of doubt no matter what. I think it's a healthy feeling because it prepares you for the worst."

These girls are realists. They know they have to work hard if they want to do well in school, if they want to go to college, and if they want to make their dreams come true. And as Bree, age seventeen, said, "Don't think anyone is going to hand-feed you. But if you work at it, you can reach your goal." Another young woman, Sarah, said, "Don't fall for the bottom of the barrel just because it looks easy."

Betty Thomas on Plugging Away

Betty Thomas has won an Emmy Award for both her acting and her directing—quite an accomplishment! Best known for her role on the TV show *Hill Street Blues*, Betty decided she wanted to try her hand at directing. When I asked her how she shifted gears, she pointed out how one skill leads to another, showing us how confidence is built on various playing fields.

"I was a shy kid. And though no one really said, 'No, you can't do such-and-such,' I still couldn't imagine how I was going to become a director. Why would anyone hire me as a director if I hadn't had any real experience? But I did learn to improvise when I was at Second City in Chicago. As an actress, I had also learned to audition and knew that directors had to audition, too. What I began to realize was that I could count on my own words, which ultimately gave me the confidence to try directing. I kept plugging away, and finally it came together for me."

Crystal Windham on Nurturing Your Talent

If you were out on the road today, chances are that Crystal Windham had a hand in designing some of the cars you passed. This young African American woman is an award-winning car designer now working for General Motors. She remembers always being interested in art and design but that her interest had to be nurtured.

"First I was told I had to have talent. I had an art teacher in tenth grade who told me and my mom that I had talent in the art field, so she led me to the College for Creative Studies, and from there I worked on different mediums. I definitely had to learn that if I loved to draw and be creative, I needed to figure out how to take that creativity and apply it."

There is tenaciousness in her voice. When I asked Crystal what advice she would give to any of you young ladies today who might share her interest in the arts, she said:

"You should surround yourselves with people who are encouraging. You should be flexible enough in attitude to hear the negatives, and always remain open-minded. You also have to be willing to do the hard work. A lot has to be said about really going with the inner feeling and passion that you're looking for, being educated about it. And then you'll find success."

NICOLE MILLER ON BEING A FIGHTER

When you see me all dressed up on the red carpet, I could be wearing a Nicole Miller gown. She's had her company for more than twenty-five years, and I love her style. I also admire her creativity and the determination she has to make it in the very fickle world of fashion. What's her secret?

"I'm a hard worker. A lot of people get stuck in a rut and become more conservative. I've never lost my focus on my customer. I'm a fighter and I don't give up."

Confidence comes from the support of your family or role models, because of a winning attitude, and it can emerge in spite of critics. Confidence is certainly what helped these inspiring women rise to the top of their fields. It's what has helped them rally at low times and soar during high times.

For me, confidence always comes from my heart. Even when times are tough, I dig deep and reach into myself, trusting that I can get through anything. Doing this over and over again has helped me try new things, test myself, and always, always keep growing. As you think about your own confidence, keep this in mind: Dig deep and trust yourself. You can do it. You can do anything.

Chapter Three

You Are the Boss

DREAM BIG AND SEE BEYOND THIS MOMENT

*I am what I am and I'll do what I want. As long as what I do
doesn't hurt anyone, I will do what I want.* —Joss Stone

I just love the phrase "Dream big!" To me it conjures up
everything that self-esteem can do for a person—building a
sense of empowerment, optimism, and confidence. Dreaming big means that you let yourself think outside the box and
that you can imagine great things for yourself. It doesn't
matter what your dream is—to be a heart surgeon, captain of
industry, or president of the United States—it all has to start
from deep within. Every big dream begins as the small notion within us that anything is possible. It starts with believing in yourself and refusing to let stereotypes stand in your
way. A seventeen-year-old from Atlanta named Chelsea put
it eloquently: "We need to know that we can dream big and

we don't have to limit ourselves—even if we are not rich, not skinny, or not boys." Talk about saying it all!

You are about to meet some more incredible women who dared to dream big and who have chosen professions that are unusual in one way or another: a race-car driver who gives the boys a run for their money; an astronaut who became the first American woman to soar into space; the girl who wrote in her eighth-grade diary that she was going to be an army officer and went on to become a general; the woman appointed as the first female fire chief in her city; the speaker of the U.S. House of Representatives who is the first woman to hold the position; and a governor who dared to dream of something unconventional.

None of these women started off thinking she would become a trailblazer. But for all of them, somewhere along the way their dreams began to get bigger and more real, and eventually they broke through barriers and became the inspirational leaders they are today.

What might you accomplish if *you* dared to dream big?

Reach for the Stars

Dreaming big isn't all about fantasy. Closing your eyes and imagining yourself belting out rock tunes in front of millions when you've never so much as sung a note—that's a fantasy. Taking singing lessons, practicing, performing in small venues, making a demo—and doing what it takes to become a true rock star—that's dreaming big. See the difference? You need to have the dream, but you need to follow it up with practice and action. You also need to give yourself the freedom to imagine limitless possibilities. Once you have a big dream, getting there is about setting goals, working hard, and taking advantage of all opportunities, no matter how small. It will sometimes mean taking a wrong turn. But even detours can end up being good for us. If you can learn from mistakes, going for your dream is what matters most.

DANICA PATRICK ON FINDING SOMETHING THAT YOU LOVE

World-famous race-car driver Danica Patrick, whom I met on the red carpet at the ESPY Awards, is a woman who exudes confidence in a field that is definitely a boys' club. She sent me this email about her philosophy when it comes to young women dreaming big and being tough:

"Set your sights as far out as you can dream, then as you grow up you will have a solid goal that will guide you up the ladder of success. Find something that you love to do and you are good at, and make a career of it. I believe that the way you get to the top is to have such a passion for something that you are willing to do anything. It's a tough road, and if you don't have the heart and desire, then you'll be tempted to give up along the way. The only difference between one person and the next is how bad you want it."

JULIANNE MOORE ON ACCOMPLISHMENTS, BIG AND SMALL

I just love watching Julianne Moore onscreen. An Academy Award–nominated and Emmy- and Golden Globe–winning actress, Moore is also a children's book author and mother. In her explanation, a "big dream" can be large or small—so long as it has value to you.

"We currently live in a culture that celebrates celebrity, appearance, even notoriety—all of which have very little content and meaning. For me, the root of self-esteem is accomplishment, both big and small. An accomplishment is something of value—whether it is the ability to make others comfortable, build something with your hands, read well for comprehension—anything, absolutely anything that you do that has meaning for you. And that you derive pleasure from! I think that many girls are misled, these days, by a culture that celebrates the superficial.

"What matters most (more than what you look like, how much you weigh, where you came from, your financial status—all those things we *think* matter) is who you are and what you care about. Find meaning in your life, search for purpose, strive toward understanding your world and contributing to it, no matter what it is. If it is of consequence to you, it is important."

Governor Kathleen Sebelius on Believing You Can Do Anything

In 2003, Kathleen Sebelius was elected the second female governor of the state of Kansas. She has become so respected in the Democratic Party that she was strongly considered as a vice presidential candidate during the '08 campaign. When I asked her if she always knew she would be in politics, she told me that she hadn't been at all sure what she was going to do with her life.

In fact, her first career aspiration was quite interesting.

"I guess my first real goal was to be a garbageman, because these folks used to come to our street in Cincinnati and drove incredibly cool trucks and they would come on Mondays and have lunch on our street so the garbage trucks would line up and the guys would get out and I would take my lunch out and sit with them—much to my mother's somewhat horror. But I thought that would be an amazing job to actually drive one of those great big trucks. There were no garbagewomen, so I really wanted to be a garbageman."

Later on, Governor Sebelius says that there were two important factors in helping her dream big and aspire to a life of public service.

"It never occurred to me that I couldn't do anything I wanted as a woman. I went to an all-girls school, from kindergarten to college. So unlike a lot of women my age, my experience was that girls did everything. They were the ballerinas, they were the jocks, they were the smartest in the class, the dumbest in the class, they were the leaders and the followers. I never was in a situation in which girls did not play all of those roles. I think that was an incredibly important life lesson for me—something that was not taught but acted upon day in and day out. I would say that the other important piece in believing I could do anything was growing up with a brother who is fifteen months older and a brother 360 days younger than me. We had a house with a big yard on the side and a basketball court out back. Most of the pickup games for baseball, football, or basketball were boys only, but I got to play because it was my house. My brothers would often be confronted by someone who would arrive for one of these games and say, 'Who is that? We don't let girls play.' My brothers would say indignantly, 'That's not a girl, that's our sister.' I just figured out through my life experience that you really can participate in anything that you're willing to show up for."

Governor Sebelius brings up my next point: that for young girls and women, dreaming big often means resisting stereotypes.

Be a She-Ro

Throughout this book, in addition to the women whose names you recognize from TV, film, and music, you will meet many others who have not only pursued careers in areas that were once off-limits to women but who have achieved amazing successes in once male-dominated fields. I think of these women as pioneers who are changing the world before our eyes. By breaking down such barriers, these women have paved the road for other women to do the same.

I am sure that many of you have a similar fierce determination to challenge and beat these female stereotypes. So, go ahead—get on the rooftops and shout, "I'm not afraid to break the mold!"

Girls Inc. Link: What Gets in Our Way

Girls Inc. found that only 13 percent of the more than two thousand girls surveyed think it is "very easy" for girls to achieve their aspirations and "become the kind of person they want to be when they grow up." Wow, think about that: That means that 87 percent of you see it as a challenge to become the best you were meant to be. Let's change that statistic!*

*"The Supergirl Dilemma: Girls Grapple with Mounting Pressure of Expectations."

QUEEN LATIFAH ON CHALLENGING HOLLYWOOD'S EXPECTATIONS

There are few people who are less afraid of challenging the limitations of stereotypes than the multitalented Queen Latifah. She is an Oscar-nominated actress, a Grammy-winning rapper, a comedienne, producer, and model.

"I knew I didn't fit the mold of what was popular in Hollywood or what was typically successful in Hollywood. But I also knew that as long as I stayed true to myself and did things that worked for me, I was always going to be happy and satisfied. For the most part, I have felt good about what I've been doing, and I am still growing and advancing in my career."

DR. SALLY RIDE ON GIRLS IN THE SCIENCES

Ride, Sally, ride! I have to admit that I was a little bit nervous when I got Dr. Sally Ride on the phone. As the first American female astronaut, she is, in my eyes, a legend, and a pioneer like no other. Can you imagine what confidence she had to have to reach such heights (literally!) in her career, especially at a time when women were not encouraged to be in the sciences? I asked Dr. Ride to zero in on just how hard it is to dream big when you're grappling with the unconscious message that your smarts don't count.

"I was a normal girl growing up in Los Angeles who preferred to be outside than inside, but I also happened to like science and math even when I was nine or ten years old. When I was in middle school and early high school, I had the same self-esteem issues that a lot of girls have, the same self-confidence issues. I was getting good grades, but I didn't think that I had the ability and the smarts to continue getting those good grades. By eleventh and twelfth grade, I had the impression that people were much smarter than I was. I began to even question whether I could go to college. *How could I ever succeed in college? How could I ever go on in science?* But at the time I was very fortunate to have two teachers in the early stages of high school who were good science teachers and spent enough time with me to start giving me confidence in myself. They said things like, 'Well, if you were good in biology in sixth grade, you'll be good in biology in twelfth grade, and you'll be good in biology in college. And if you were good in math in fifth grade, you'll be good in math in eleventh grade, and you'll be good in math in college.' These were things I really needed to hear, or I'm certain I would not have followed the path that I did."

Rabbi Laura Geller on Making History

One of the most inspirational women I talked to for this book was Laura Geller of Temple Emanuel in Beverly Hills. She was the fourth woman in the United States to become an ordained rabbi. She told me about the stereotypes she faced when she entered the seminary and how other women actually helped her stay focused on her dream.

"When I was young, there were no women [rabbis] to serve as role models for me. But the fact that there weren't any women in my class and only one other woman in the seminary at the time didn't deter me because it didn't really occur to me that being a woman would be a barrier.

"Once I was in seminary, I began to understand the extent to which I was actually transgressing by studying to be a rabbi. Many people thought I was there only to find a husband. . . . So along the way there were many challenges and also many blessings. One of the things that was really helpful to me when I began the program was to recognize that there were women who weren't studying to be rabbis but who wanted to understand what being Jewish meant to them. These women became my friends and support group."

Carolyn Porco on Never Giving Up

If you've ever seen some really cool pictures of the planet Saturn, then you may be able to thank Carolyn Porco, a planetary scientist who was the leader of NASA's *Cassini* orbiter, which circled and took images of the ringed planet. What a trailblazer!

"I don't think that women bring any more or less native brainpower or mental acumen to the study of anything. But still, in our world, women and men are raised to behave differently, and so they tend to conduct themselves differently, with males in general being more aggressive and women in general being more conscientious and careful. I am blessed to have several women working within my organization, women on whom I can rely to do very careful work. In conducting spaceflight operations, these characteristics are essential."

Even though Ms. Porco had strong female role models who helped her believe that as a woman she could do anything, she wasn't always so sure of her path. Like many of us, she had moments of self-doubt and indecision, and spent time following other pursuits before her career became clear to her.

"I have gone through many times when I was in fact paralyzed by self-doubt. My first attempt at doing a doctoral dissertation failed. I even left graduate school for a year and lived in the mountains of Colorado, in a log cabin, chopping wood, making apple butter, and earning a living being a part-time computer programmer. But my desire to make something of myself, to follow my passion, and to lead a meaningful existence was, thankfully, strong enough to override any self-doubt. I also had a mother who, despite a very hard and frustrated life, was a very positive thinker and didn't let things stand in her way. So that attitude rubbed off on me. And after a year, I went back to graduate school and worked on a completely different topic—Saturn's rings. Basically, I just refused to quit; a quitter wasn't what I wanted to be. Accomplishing something was important enough to me to give it everything I had, to make what sacrifices needed to be made to be successful. And it worked. Completing my dissertation gave me the confidence to move on to greater challenges."

Trisha Wilson on Not Being Intimidated

My friend Trisha Wilson started her own architectural-design firm and has created and installed more than a million guest rooms in some of the world's most luxurious hotels. She's definitely a pioneer in this male-dominated field.

"Having been a woman business owner since my early twenties, I have often found myself as the only woman at the table during a business meeting. I have dealt with that situation in two ways: (1) I always speak my mind (I refuse to be intimidated!); and (2) I never question myself—I have confidence in myself and I *know* I can do it!

"One experience stands out in my mind. In 1991 I became the first woman to serve as president of the local chapter of YPO (Young Presidents' Organization). The men weren't sure what kind of gift to give a female president, so they gave me a man's tie to wear! I thought it was so funny that instead of celebrating this milestone for the organization (which women would have done), they gave me a gift to help me blend in as 'one of the guys'! I wasn't intimidated at being the only 'girl' in the group, because I always just *knew* I could do it.

"During the course of my career I have seen so many barriers for women broken down. Like other women in my generation, I have been able to achieve things that my mother and grandmother never could have dreamed of doing. I hope that the young women who are coming along today will appreciate that there are virtually no barriers for them, and they can do and achieve anything they want to do!"

You go, girl!

Even though women have abundant choices—and can break barriers to make still more choices available—we still have a long way to go to see that women are treated as equal to men. My friends who are actresses say that it is still difficult for a woman to "open" or be the main star of a movie. They don't get paid as much as their male counterparts and are often relegated to roles in which they are just "eye candy." So as females, we need to demand that that change. We need to support films and television shows that feature strong female roles. When we buy our music, we need to be conscious that the lyrics don't degrade women (even if we just like the beat). These are ways that you can be involved in making advancements for women in the entertainment industry and beyond. Show everyone that you have a voice.

Patricia Handy on Becoming a Conductor

For me there are few things more relaxing than listening to classical music. Conducting an orchestra is still mostly a man's world, but Patricia Handy is a pioneer who knows how to make beautiful music; she has been the associate conductor of the Greenwich Symphony Orchestra since 1979. She shared her story about how and why she became an orchestra conductor. Talk about paving her own way!

"I was drawn to become a conductor because I was frequently in ensembles and I would sit there thinking that the piece should be orchestrated another way. I didn't like the way the music was being interpreted. Then it became obvious to me that if I wanted the piece to go the way I wanted it to go, I had to become a conductor. I originally wanted to be a choral conductor because women were able to do that. That's more accepted for a woman, but I became very attracted to the orchestral repertoires, so I just moved into that. At the time, there were no women conductors. None. They didn't exist. So I was in the very first wave of women who tried, and that was a very hard place to be.

"People were trying to discourage me, of course. And there was certainly no guidance whatsoever. But I just was determined to do it myself. I felt I had to do it. It was such a compelling voice in me that kept telling me to keep on going no matter what happens. And people along the way were not saying, 'Hey, this is great what you're doing! What can I do to help?' Not at all! People were brutal to me. Even after I was in.

"I worked with Leonard Bernstein for a while, and . . . he was the only one who was really kind. Otherwise, people would question me: 'What are you doing? This is wrong!' I was in my mid-twenties and I sort of thought, well, I must be talented because of the competitive programs to which I'd been accepted. So finally I just decided, well, I must be good or these people wouldn't be paying for me! So that was it."

Nancy O'Dell on Not Giving In

Nancy O'Dell has been my colleague and friend for ten years. She is an Emmy Award–winning journalist and host of *Access Hollywood*. She's also a mom who spends much of her time working with charitable organizations. She really captured the essence of dreaming big and challenging those barriers when she said:

> "I think one of the most important lessons for girls to learn is to not give in to or accept stereotypical ideas. How great was the 2008 presidential election in that we had both Hillary Clinton as a contender for the Democratic presidential candidate and Sarah Palin as the VP Republican candidate? Those are the highest positions held in this country, so don't let anything hold *you* back! Take on leadership positions in your school. Play sports. . . . Girls can be just as competitive as boys. . . . Sports also teach you a valuable lesson: Never give up! Some of the biggest success stories I have heard are from those people who were told no, but didn't accept that answer and went on to do great things."

Putting in Your Time

By the time I was in college, I had made up my mind that I was going to become a television journalist. And because I showed so much interest, a teacher asked me if I wanted to try out for the hosting position for a very small local cable show. I jumped at the chance even if they didn't pay me— I just wanted the experience.

I remember my very first day on the job so clearly. I was interviewing a couple of people about a community event, and I was looking at my notes more than my guests. I had never read a teleprompter and was a little stiff in my delivery. But the producer said I showed a lot of promise—and that did so much for my self-esteem. Then, during the summers of my junior and senior years, I went back home to Detroit and interned at a local television station. I was able to go out on assignments with the veteran reporters and learn how to put a good story together. Slowly, I got a chance to do some on-camera work myself and started putting a résumé tape together, and eventually the station hired me to be a reporter and anchor. Now, the internship wasn't a paid position and even when I got hired, it was part-time and the station wasn't paying much at all. But staying with these jobs kept me on the path to achieving my big dream. To make the money I needed to live while pursuing that dream, I registered with a temp agency that helped me find office work like answering phones and filing (which I was very good at, by the way!) during the hours I wasn't working in TV.

A lot of times the media will talk about someone being an "overnight sensation." It will often appear that an actor or singer has become famous in the blink of an eye, making the rest of us feel like our success is very slow in coming. But after working in the entertainment business for years, I know there is no such thing as an overnight sensation. For people who are truly talented—those who have really accomplished something—they will tell you that hard work and paying your dues is just part of the deal and that the earlier you start, the better. But if you don't know exactly what you want to do after school, don't beat yourself up. Just start small and build toward what interests you. Dr. Sally Ride offers some more advice in this area.

Dr. Sally Ride on Taking Baby Steps

....

"Sometimes it's difficult to generate that motivation entirely from within. You need to look around and realize that there are an infinite number of opportunities for you as you grow older, in a variety of different areas. These days you can literally do whatever you want to do. You can be a news anchor, you can be an astronaut, you can be a scientist studying whether there might be primitive life on Mars, or you can be an environmental scientist. You can literally be any number of things and follow a path that you choose that really appeals to you.

"You really have to start down [a] road fairly early, not in deciding exactly what you want to do—no one does that—but building a foundation in your schoolwork and in your personal skills, so that you can collaborate with people and work as part of a team. These skills will enable you to take advantage of opportunities as you grow older. There's really no better way to do that than to find examples of people—a teacher, or a parent, or an older brother, older sister, cousin, or uncle—who can be an example to you and talk to you about what they went through growing up. But if [you don't know someone personally], look at examples of other women who have been successful and you'll find that growing up, they were normal people. They didn't always know what they wanted to do; in fact, usually they didn't know what they wanted to do until they got a little older. But they were able to find it within themselves to build that foundation that allowed them to take advantage of the opportunities later."

Many of the girls in my task-force groups spoke about their plans in a *big* way. The girls from Atlanta had just graduated from high school and had big plans: One wanted to be a surgical nurse, another wanted to be a veterinarian, another wanted to be a heart surgeon, and another wanted to be a neurosurgeon—quite a group of future medics! Even with the similarities in their imagined professions, their dreams are as wide and varied as the girls themselves.

Although some of these girls might one day change their minds, the fact that they feel focused now enables them to prioritize their time, making sure they get good grades and take classes that help prepare them for the field of medicine. In this way, they'll be able to determine if their career goals are really right for them.

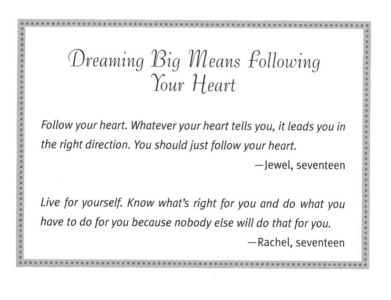

Dreaming Big Means Following Your Heart

Follow your heart. Whatever your heart tells you, it leads you in the right direction. You should just follow your heart.

—Jewel, seventeen

Live for yourself. Know what's right for you and do what you have to do for you because nobody else will do that for you.

—Rachel, seventeen

Stay Strong

As focused as the group from Atlanta seemed, many of the girls in my task-force groups were anxious about their futures. They were trying hard and doing well in school, but they weren't sure what to study in college or do with their lives. If you're feeling the same way, it's important to remember that even the most successful women I talked to had to try a few things out before they found their passion.

EVA MENDES ON REJECTION

That was definitely the case for actress Eva Mendes. You might have seen her gracing the red carpet at one of her big movie premieres. Eva told me that she feels like she has grown into being a very confident woman. It's also clear that she knows about being persistent and going after your dreams.

"I really had to work on my self-esteem. I come from a working-class family (that means no money!), so my options were limited, but I realized that I had to find something that I was good at and that I loved to do. I didn't figure out what that was until I was twenty-three, but the journey of trying to find myself gave me the self-confidence I needed. I remember trying out for volleyball, and I was awful! So, I moved on to drill team—and was kicked off! I have a lot of rejection stories, but I persevered. How? By surrounding myself with positive people who supported me, no matter the outcome. Thankfully, I had a good family, but for those of you who don't, please realize that we can't choose our family, but we can choose our friends. Surrounding myself with people who love and support me has been my key to success. Once I eliminated the negative people from my circle, I was ready to soar."

GENERAL VELMA RICHARDSON ON FOLLOWING A PATH AND IGNORING THE NAYSAYERS

Retired U.S. army general Velma "Von" Richardson gained the reputation in the army of being tough but fair and someone who always encouraged her troops to be their personal best. She said that women were not encouraged to go into the service at the time she enlisted. But that didn't stop this African American gal from Bennettsville, South Carolina, from pursuing her passion.

"I can't say that I ever dreamed about becoming a general, but I had an aunt who joined the army the year I was born. I was impressed with her and wanted to follow in her footsteps. In eighth grade I decided that I would become an army officer. I remember writing my aspirations about what I wanted to do in my life in my diary: 'I plan to be an army officer.' My girlfriends, in particular, really laughed at me. Maybe something was just a little bit wrong with me, but I had seen my aunt and we certainly didn't grow up with a lot, and so my aunt certainly appeared to have more than anyone in Bennettsville, South Carolina. Of course when she joined the army, it was the Women's Army Corps (WAC). And when I joined the army, I joined the WAC. It wasn't until a couple years later that there was a full transition of the Women's Army Corps into the regular army."

Although General Richardson had a role model in her aunt, she also confronted criticism, doubts, and questions—her friends even made fun of her. How did she manage those contrary voices?

"Doing what you want and following your heart takes an awful lot of tenacity. I certainly do care about what people think of me. I do care whether or not people are supportive—especially when they should be. There are also a number of things that need to fall into place for all of that to work. My thing was, okay, I'm fairly bright, I'm capable, and while I need your support, I probably will do well with the minimum, and just do extra work on my own. That's what I did. You can imagine, [their doubts and criticism] hurt my feelings, not to the point where I cried, but I thought to myself, *You have to get past this,* and I did."

CAROLYN PORCO ON PERSEVERANCE

Carolyn Porco, the planetary scientist, also tried to block out the naysayers. She persevered and ultimately succeeded.

"The best thing you can do is to not care what others think about you. Ignore the incessant, obnoxious, ubiquitous, and blaring external messages telling you what you should look like, act like, be like. Discover what matters to you, what motivates you, what pleases you, what makes your life meaningful. Then go for it, and simply ignore all other distractions, including any friends and family members who may try to steer you otherwise. You need to learn how to turn disadvantages to advantages, make lemonade out of lemons—these are very useful skills in life."

SPEAKER NANCY PELOSI ON WHAT'S POSSIBLE

All eyes have been on Madame Speaker, Nancy Pelosi, since she was elected the first female speaker of the House in 2006. But before all that, she was a young girl challenging the stereotypes of her day. Clearly, never giving up has served her well.

> "As the only girl in a Catholic Italian American family with five older brothers, I was raised in a protective home, where girls were not encouraged to take risks. There were many expectations about how women should act and their role in the home. Now, years later, as a mother raising five children, I never imagined that I would go from the kitchen to the Congress, and eventually become the first woman speaker of the House of Representatives. When I first was elected into the House leadership, I received letters from around the world, including many from young girls. I was particularly touched by one from a young woman who quoted Eleanor Roosevelt saying, 'The future belongs to those who believe in the beauty of their dreams.' That was as true then as it is now. I understand the difficulties and challenges young girls face growing up today. To these young girls who are not yet confident in their abilities and talents I say: 'You may not realize it now, but you have the power to make your dreams a reality. Never give up. Anything is possible. If you remain focused on achieving your goal, you will succeed and realize your full potential.'"

Tracy Jarman on Staying the Course

Tracy Jarman, San Diego's first female fire chief, has been a firefighter for more than twenty years, recognized nationally for her service in the industry. I asked her what she would say to the girls who would want to pursue a profession that is traditionally seen as a man's job. She said:

> "Number one, don't let anyone ever tell you that you can't do something. And then, you need to be patient. The young women of

today are used to fast foods, the Internet and text messaging and instant service, and I think they need to realize it takes a lot of hard work and dedication to realize your dream. You need to stay focused on your goal, and it takes time. It doesn't happen overnight. It took me over two years to become a firefighter from the time I decided I was going to go after it. It's not going to happen instantaneously. You need to hold on to it and stay focused."

Joss Stone on Staying Strong

Best New Artist nominee Joss Stone, an indie rocker and Grammy winner who has sold more than ten million albums worldwide, sums up the idea of dreaming big perfectly.

"Being a young woman is one of the most difficult things in any kind of business. If you're trying to do something and succeed, a lot of people around you will be like, 'No, no, no—you need help with this, you need help with that.' That's not the case with most young men. For a woman, it's hard to get that respect. Most of the businessmen I encounter don't see the strengths in a woman. I want to tell them, we are completely equal. So you have to be strong and do what you say you're going to do. If you say you're going to go out there and do something, you do it—without any hesitation. And if people are underestimating you, then just take them out of the equation. Don't even invite them into your world."

Don't you just love that inspiration from Joss Stone? As young women, you have probably been told somewhere along the way that there are limitations for you—a glass ceiling that will prevent you from achieving your dreams.

You may have heard this directly or through subliminal messages that our society sends every day. However, the presidential primaries of 2008, when Hillary Clinton ran for the Democratic nomination, proved that women are making giant cracks in that glass ceiling and, more and more often, breaking right through. So begin to envision yourself doing big things. Bring your goals into sharp focus and give your dreams everything you've got!

Chapter Four

· · · · · · · ·

You Are Different

THINK FOR YOURSELF AND CHOOSE
FRIENDS WISELY

Very early on, I became my own best friend.

— DIANE VON FURSTENBERG

I've learned so much listening and talking to young women like you about how complicated life is for your generation, especially when it comes to social life. When I was a teenager, we didn't have cell phones, so in addition to not being able to reach people on the phone all the time, there was no text messaging. The Internet was barely on the horizon, so there was no Facebook or MySpace to connect with twenty thousand "friends" at one time. Your world is so much bigger and faster than mine was when I was in school.

But what I'm also hearing from you is that as different as the world is now, the pressure to fit in and belong has largely remained the same. Many of you, in one way or another, still feel "isolated," "different," or "like an outsider," even if you have the latest celebrity jeans, iPod, or dozens of cyber buddies you connect with on a daily basis.

There is no place that puts more pressure on a person to fit in and, at the same time, excludes them than Hollywood. You've heard of the lists in this town—the A-list, B-list, and so on. I go to a lot of events as part of my job, and I'm also invited as a guest when I'm not working. Playing the social circuit, so to speak, is fast-paced and very exciting, but sometimes it can leave me feeling strangely uncomfortable. You can be around a thousand people and still feel very alone, not really a part of anything here in Hollywood. While there are plenty of very decent and interesting people who simply like to mingle at these events, there are also many who seem to *need* to be at every function, hobnobbing with stars all the time. I find these folks are missing something inside. It's as if they have to be connected to the rich and famous just to feel important. They want to fit in so badly that they've forgotten that they have something to offer, too.

How can we all handle the pressure to fit in, while staying true to who we are in our hearts?

Feeling Different

When I was in high school, I desperately wanted a Louis Vuitton satchel handbag. There was a clique of very popular girls whose families had money, and they always dressed really nicely, with lots of gold chains (the Mr. T look was in back then) and really expensive purses and shoes. Of course, I wanted to fit in with this group—they always seemed to be having a good time—but my family couldn't spend lots of money on pricey clothing. I had nice things, but I definitely didn't shop at the top-of-the-line stores. After I begged and begged, my dad finally got me the LV bag for Christmas, even though it was a financial sacrifice for him to do so. I will never forget the first day I carried my new purse to school. This one really popular girl—I'll call her Anne—who seemed to have every-designer-everything, caught a glimpse of my new purse and stared at it very closely to see if it was a fake. I positioned the bag in front of me so she could get a really good look. When she realized it was real and not a knockoff, she rolled her eyes as if to say, "How could *she* afford that?"

Just recently, my best friend from high school, Sherri, and I were reminiscing about people we went to school with and Anne's name came up. I was really surprised when Sherri told me that Anne was now struggling to make ends meet. I said, "I thought her family was rich." "Noooooo," Sherri told me. "They never had much money. They were only really good at pretending they did." She went on to tell me that *everyone* (except me, obviously) knew that Anne and her family would buy expensive clothes and cars even though they could not afford them and over the years it all resulted in debt that grew to the size of a mountain. Their rich lifestyle wasn't real, it was an image they were trying to project. And I fell for it. Here I was, trying to impress Anne, and she was just as broke as I was!

Even if I hadn't figured Anne out, I'm sure that I was not alone in trying to fit in when I was young. It's likely that everyone else out there was secretly trying to fit in, no matter the cost. And today it's no different. "Girls want to feel that they are normal and accepted for who they are," said Megan, age thirteen. "All these feelings that we are going through, we want to know that other people are feeling them, too." Figuring out who you are amidst the pressures to be like everyone else and be part of the in crowd is never easy, but I definitely think it helps to know, as Megan said so beautifully, that we're *all* privately trying to find our way through these tricky waters.

Eva Mendes on Feeling Socially Inept

As Eva Mendes said to me, feeling different often means feeling "less than."

"The most challenging time in my life was between the ages of thirteen and eighteen. I felt physically awkward and socially inept. I was so insecure about not only how I looked but also about everything I said. I second-guessed myself constantly. At that time, in my school, being of Latin descent wasn't yet considered cool. In fact, it was kind of looked down upon, so I would often lie about my origins. It was a difficult time for me because I only wanted to belong, and the harder I tried, the more I was rejected."

Céline Dion on Not Blending In

International superstar Céline Dion has won multiple Grammy Awards as well as many awards in her native Canada and in Europe. She graciously granted me an interview while she was jetting between press events during a wildly packed publicity tour. She described vivid memories of feeling like she didn't fit in when she was a young girl.

"Growing up it was very difficult. As the youngest of fourteen children, I always wanted to be around my mom and family because I felt protected by them, but I never felt like I was blending in with the other kids. They had the jean of the moment and we couldn't afford jeans or really any nice clothing, which made me feel like I was never very pretty. I was also very, very skinny, and I was not good in school."

VIRGINIA MADSEN ON STANDING UP
TO THE IN CROWD

Who could imagine that the fabulously and proudly unique Oscar-nominated and Golden Globe–nominated actress Virginia Madsen was once unpopular? She shared with me an inspiring story about one particularly heartbreaking experience that many of you will be able to relate to.

"As a teenager, there were times of such loneliness that even though I had my few girlfriends, I felt an incredible amount of rejection—rejection from boys, rejection from girls. I remember a day when I had a good pep talk with a grown-up in my life because I felt isolated at lunch. The lunch period is torture for a kid. It's really hard. So this adult said to me, 'You know what? You should just go and get your lunch and sit down at the popular table. Just sit down with those girls.'

"So I thought about that for a long time and said, 'You know what? You're right.' I felt really cool that day. I was wearing my cork platform sandals, and I had tried hard to straighten my hair (my hair is really kinky and curly, and at that time it was really not cool to have curly hair). Can you see how long I was preparing for this moment? So I just got my tray of terrible lunchroom food, and I just walked up to the popular table where they were all seated, and they all stopped talking and looked at me as I walked up. And I just sat right down at their table and said, 'Hey! How ya doin'?' Very nonchalant trying to eat my lunch, and one girl at the end of the table said, 'What is that doing here?' I wasn't paying attention, so I just ate, and I don't even remember what they were saying. I think I just tuned it out because I was just going to be really happy and hang out, and I thought if they just got to know me, they would be my friends. And then one by one they each got up from the table, very deliberately, and one by one left.

"I sat there in the middle of the lunchroom. This was a huge school with a couple of thousand students with a big giant gymnasium-sized lunchroom, and mine was the only table that had only one person at it: me. But as devastated as I was, I sat there trying to look happy and very slowly enjoy my lunch. I ate everything, even the horrible creamed corn, and after I finished all of it I took my time with my napkin. And when I was good and ready, I got up and walked away, past all the other tables all the way to the garbage cans, where I dumped my garbage and proudly walked out the door. Of course directly from there, I went down into the basement of the school and sobbed.

"I was not going to give up my pride. I was not going to let them humiliate me, even then I knew that in that moment, I would not let anyone humiliate me. And that was kind of a lesson. In my mind it was a pretty dramatic story. It's a scene in a movie that you'd say, 'Oh that would never happen,' but it really taught me something about myself. I may crumble inside, but no one has the right to humiliate me. But I did tell my mom when I went home. A lot of times we don't tell. A lot of times something really horrible can happen to girls and they don't tell because they're scared of being humiliated, they're scared of being embarrassed, and they're scared it's going to get worse. But I told. I told my mom, and it was not like she could do a lot in that situation, but I felt better after talking to her."

Virginia's story says a lot about how hard it is to be a teenager, especially if you're having trouble belonging to the in crowd. Let's face it: They are called "mean girls" for a reason. But it also highlights her strength of character and her perseverance—she turned to those she could count on—a teacher and her mother. She didn't withdraw into isolation, even if she felt so alone. In other words, she took care of herself. And that made all the difference.

A number of the girls from my task force shared similar kinds of experiences. Like Ali, age fourteen, who told me, "I used to live in a smaller city where people didn't really judge you. Everyone was popular. Everyone was friends with each other. Here, I said something wrong to one girl who was my friend, and all of a sudden, her friends decided they weren't going to be my friend. It's so different than what I was used to."

And Beth, age seventeen, said, "I'm an actress and a model. I heard some of the rumors behind my back. They were like, 'She can't be a model, she's not even pretty.' When people put me down, it hurts, and I try to cover it up with laughing or telling a joke."

Girls can be mean and immature about difference, which makes it hard sometimes to listen to your own voice. Whether because of our race or ethnicity, the neighborhood in which we grew up, our emerging sexual orientation, or our body type, most of us have felt different at one time in our lives. We can feel different from or not part of the crowd for many reasons, but it's what we do with that feeling that matters.

JULIE CHEN ON EMBRACING HER DIFFERENCE

As the anchor of CBS's *Early Show* and host of *Big Brother,* Julie Chen is another journalist who knows how media images can really affect a girl's self-esteem. She also had painful experiences from this time in her life, but eventually she came to see her difference as an asset, not a drawback.

"I can recall growing up and feeling isolated and odd for being different because of my race. Being only one of three Asian kids in my class made me feel different. I thought different was holding me back from opportunities. It wasn't until I was in my late twenties when a very wise woman, my feng shui master, who is like a life coach to me, told me being different makes me special. She said being Asian is not holding me back from reaching new heights in my career. If I were to embrace it, it would only help. She was right."

Turning It Around

Here's the good news: feeling different does *not* have to mean feeling less than. Many of the women in this book have the benefit of experience and wisdom, and their insights into how to transform feelings of isolation and not fitting in into a strong sense of self are awe-inspiring.

Martina Navratilova on "Normal"

A champion on and off the tennis court, Martina Navratilova has been called one of the greatest athletes of the century. She was ranked the number-one tennis player in the world for seven years. But even someone as successful as Martina is not immune to feeling different—in her case, it was because of her sexual orientation. However, as she explains, your difference doesn't have to be a negative.

"I was nineteen when I had my first sexual experience with a woman, though I realized I'd had feelings prior to that—crushes since I was about eight or nine. But I had no idea what they were. I liked boys okay, but women took my breath away. So after that first night I just thought, *Oh boy, my life just got a lot more complicated.* But other than that I had no real hang-ups about it. I think for a lot of kids and people religion really gets in the way; so I was lucky because that was not the case, as I grew up in a communist country and being religious was not really an option. But I remember distinctly that I always thought homosexuality was okay; I never saw a problem with it and did not understand why others did.

"If I am nothing else now, I am comfortable in my own skin. You just have to trust it. . . . Being different is just that. We need to celebrate diversity and differences. Otherwise, life would really be boring. A friend of mine once told me, 'After all, normal is just a cycle on the washing machine.' "

Laila Ali on Being Her Own Person

Laila Ali—ever strong and powerful both in and out of the boxing ring—recognized that being different is actually another way of being exceptional. During our phone conversation, Laila told me:

"I just remember always being my own person. I can remember liking the fact that I was different. I was always taller, and you know, a lot of times young girls slump their shoulders and aren't really confident being tall because everyone else isn't, but I always liked being different, I always liked going against the crowd. I've always been a leader, not a follower. I thought it was cool to be different. A lot of kids wanted to fit in, and I never tried to do that. I remember from a very early age being that way, not caring so much what people thought, and I had an understanding from early on that everyone had their own opinion, so why does everyone else's opinion mean more than mine, you know?"

HEATHER MILLS ON FEELING LONG AND GANGLY

Philanthropist, human-rights activist, model, mom, Heather Mills wears many hats. Having lost one of her legs in a motorbike accident at twenty-five years of age, she inspired countless amputees when she took on the challenge of competing for a trophy on *Dancing with the Stars*. Wanting to encourage girls not to let imperfections keep them back, she told me how having acne as a teenager made her feel awkward and different from others, but now, as an adult, even having lost her leg doesn't get in the way of her accepting herself, just as she is.

"I had severe acne for most of my teenage life, and I was put on prescriptions for it twice. And even though I am forty now, and it all seems a long time ago, it did affect me. As I got older, I began to work more on my attributes.

"What people don't get sometimes is that I don't really think twice about my leg. It's just a leg—it's not who I am. I've always been comfortable with that. And that's what people forget. They hang out with me for a while and I'll pop my leg off and they'll just go *Oh!* Or my leg will get sore and I'll walk a bit slower. I don't make a big deal of it. And when you don't make a big deal of something, neither does anybody else. I'm so relaxed with my body now that it's hard to remember how awkward I used to feel."

GABRIELLE UNION ON BEING HERSELF

"There have been so many times in my life that I've not felt as good as others. My whole life has been a struggle of feeling less than everybody else. When I was young, I had buckteeth and couldn't close my mouth. I sucked my thumb until I was twelve—talk about self-esteem issues! But sucking my thumb was my security blanket, and I didn't stop until I finally got braces. And mind you, when I got braces, because my overbite and buckteeth were so severe, I had headgear, neck gear, and rubber bands that I had to wear all the time."

But as Gabrielle points out, even though she felt different, she still managed to be popular and have friends. The key was her confidence.

"I was in the popular group in elementary school, junior high, and high school, but I never felt like I was fully accepted. I always felt like I was this outsider. So imagine you're in the in crowd but you've got headgear, neck gear, and rubber bands. And I was always the black girl surrounded by the most beautiful blondes, with perfect bodies and gorgeous blue eyes, who are also perfect athletes—all the things that people wanted. And I was so not that. . . . I felt even more on the outside and constantly chasing this ideal of perfection that I was never going to be. I was never going to be white, I was never going to be blond, I was never going to have blue eyes. . . .

"I am still struggling. I'm in my thirties and I still have moments of low self-esteem. But I've just had to realize that I am who I am, and to find the people who love me for being exactly the person that I was born to be. Everything that I've achieved in this life I've achieved being exactly who I am—not being somebody else or trying to be somebody else. And once you do that, people are drawn to your confidence. The second you embrace who you are, the second you hop off that merry-go-round and stop chasing something that you will never be, that's when you notice that your world changes. That people are drawn to confidence. Not looks, not even popularity, none of that. If you look at the most popular girls, they are generally the most confident even if they're faking it. It's this confidence that they have that people are drawn to. It's your lack of confidence that people are trying to shy away from. Most people want to be associated with people who hold their head up high and walk tall and are confident and proud."

Candace Parker on Knowing Right from Wrong

At six feet four inches, Olympic basketball star Candace Parker had moments growing up when she felt physically awkward and out of place. But she did something remarkably smart: She tapped into the confidence she felt on the basketball court and used it to develop a rock-solid center within herself, something she could access both on and off the court. When I asked her how she handled peer pressure in high school when it started to get really intense, she said:

"I was never really into peer pressure because at an early age, I developed a conscience and knew right from wrong. It's hard to go against the norm, but oftentimes, the norm passes and you're the last one standing. That's the most important thing. You follow your morals and your guidelines and don't transform those for anyone. I know this sounds old-school, but really, are you important to them? If they don't share your likes and dislikes, then sometimes it's not cool to say no or go against the norm, but it's right. Those friends will pass. It's the ones that share your likes and dislikes and share the same morals and values that are keepers."

Facebook/MySpace/YouTube

You have access to one another in far more intense—and inva-sive—ways than ever before; technology is a constant in your lives and often is the primary way you talk to one another. But despite privacy rules and other ways to protect yourself, some girls still feel they have to join in by posting compromising pho-tos or revealing information about themselves. You have to be smarter than that. Remember that you can't take back what you post on the Internet; it is there for the world to see, *forever*. I have reported on too many stories where young ladies post a risqué picture that they think is only for the eyes of their friends, but then a jealous girl or ex-boyfriend makes the photos public. Taking photos like that, in the first place, is a risk; *anyone* can get their hands on them. A potential employer or a college admissions officer could see the photos, and you might not get the job or acceptance into the school you want.

I have both a MySpace and Facebook page, and as a per-son in the public eye, I have to be very protective about what I am putting out there for the world to see. And you should, too. Remember, not everyone is who they seem to be online, and even your friends are not always as trustworthy with your pri-vacy as you'd expect them to be. Protect your privacy like you would your most valuable possession—because it is!

Friend or Frenemy?

Sometimes it's hard to tell who our true friends really are. Although many of the girls in my task-force groups spoke about their close friendships, many also revealed that these relationships are complicated. One of the greatest lessons I have learned in my life is realizing that nothing is as important as surrounding myself with honest, supportive, and caring people. In high school, many times it was all about being with the popular group. In Hollywood, many people want to be invited to certain parties just so they can associate with people they feel are important. For me, there is a true separation between what I do for a living and how I enjoy spending my personal time. It's not that popular or famous people aren't honest and caring—and I have many good friends who are also famous—but I choose to spend time with people who I like on the inside, regardless of their outer fame.

The hard truth is that not everyone is meant to be your friend. The popular girl may know all about the parties or may be your ticket into a world that you think is more exciting than where you find yourself, but these things don't make her your friend. Make sure you know the difference.

As an adult, I've learned to enjoy my own company and experience new things away from a crowd of people who don't have the same kinds of morals that I do or who don't necessarily have my best interests at heart. At first it might seem lonely, but I've learned that when I spend time with myself, I have the opportunity to appreciate my own self-worth and really focus on goals I want to accomplish. Trust me on this: You are far better off in your own company than in that of fair-weather friends who chip away at your self-esteem. If someone doesn't make you feel good about who you are, no matter what glittery things they might offer on the surface, a "friendship" with that person will exact way too high a price.

My circle of friends has changed in the last few years. I

have weeded out those people who want to be around me because I'm on TV, those who constantly criticize other people, those whose values don't fall in line with my own. I have reconnected with trusted old friends who knew me long before I was on television and made new friends who are kind and challenge me to be a better person. And as a result, I have developed a great supportive group of people I love being around. My advice is this: Trust your instincts. Chances are you already know which friends in your life are true blue, and those are the ones worth keeping.

GARCELLE BEAUVAIS ON POPULARITY

"I always say the girls who are popular now are normally not the girls who are successful in life because they rely too much on their looks and their popularity. It's best to know who you are, be around friends who know who they are. And if being in a popular group makes you uncomfortable, don't be in that group. Find another group or join a sport team or run for class president. Know who you are, know what you like, and find friends who have the same values as you."

CÉLINE DION ON PEOPLE WHO TELL YOU THE TRUTH

Always so poised and thoughtful, Céline Dion said it well: "Make sure you choose good friends and that those friends tell you the truth. It's very easy to say to people, 'You're beautiful and you're making the right choices,' but it's very important to choose good people to tell you the truth."

Remember what Eva Mendes said about the importance of having good friends for your self-esteem? "We can choose our friends. Surrounding myself with people who love and support me has been my key to success. Once I eliminated the negative people from my circle, I was ready to soar."

Virginia Madsen on Lasting Friendships

"You must have a strong support system. You can't have fake friends. I so desperately wanted to be liked. I wanted to be popular. But I had three friends that are still my friends today. I really allowed myself to ask for help when I needed it, and we all did that for each other—it was very healthy. I think that you need to look to your sisters for assistance and support. It's incredibly important."

Alicia Keys on Going Against the Grain

"All of us are different. That's what makes us interesting and special. I don't want to be anything like another person. I want to be totally myself and go against the grain, forge my own path. I've learned that being different is what makes you stand out. It makes everything so much more intriguing."

Whether it's choosing who you want to hang out with or trying to squelch those feelings of being different—inside or out—all of us have felt uncomfortable at one time or another during our lives. But when you embrace your true self, you will always end up feeling comfortable in your own skin. And this will become yet another way to grow your self-esteem and make it as natural as waking up in the morning with a smile on your face.

Chapter Five

• • • • • • • •

You Are Human

MANAGE STRESS AND TAKE CARE OF YOURSELF

The saving thing is always laughter. —DIANE SAWYER

We've talked about the pressure to be pretty and thin. But as so many of the girls in my discussion groups have told me, there's also enormous pressure to be smart and cool and to fit in. You want to be "perfect" in so many ways, you want to meet the expectations of your family and friends, and you want to be what the media tells you you should be.

When it came to school, many of the girls in my task-force groups complained that their academic load was too heavy, even in ninth grade. They were constantly worried about their grades and spoke about how much pressure their parents put on them to do well in school so they could get into a good college. At the same time, they struggled with the demands of being popular, which means your social calendar has to be full. And of course, there is that ever-present pressure to look good, if not perfect, all the time. Do you recognize yourself in any of these comments?

Most of the pressure I have is academic. You want to please your parents, your teachers, and your friends. I never really focus on what I want.   —BETH, SEVENTEEN

My stress started right after eighth grade. My school is really competitive. When I became a freshman, they were already asking me what college I want to attend. I felt stupid because I had no idea.   —KARA, FIFTEEN

Already they are giving us a list of colleges and the expectations. You must have over a 4.0 to get in. There is so much pressure.
                    —ALI, FOURTEEN

When I started my freshman year, I had club soccer, cross-country, track, and school on top of that. There is so much pressure to do well in all of these things.   —TINA, FIFTEEN

A lot of people say that I'm smart, and they have high expectations for me. And when I sometimes fail, I'm afraid I'll fail again, and I don't want to disappoint people.
                    —LORRAINE, SIXTEEN

It must be so hard! It seemed so much more straightforward to get good grades when I was in school. A B+ average would make you a contender for most colleges, and we certainly didn't start preparing when we were in eighth grade! We didn't need an appointment book to keep up with all our after-school activities. We had much more time to chill and have fun. But let's face it, your world is much more competitive and fast-paced, and you might feel that if you make a pit stop, you will be out of the race completely. What is important, though, is that you maintain a balance and learn what good pressure is and what's the type that is not enhancing your life in any way.

Diane von Furstenberg on a Good Kind of Pressure

Diane von Furstenberg, who built a fashion empire based on her famous, signature wrap dress, told me about the drive her family created in her when she was growing up. She used her mother's challenging history as a way to help keep her own troubles—and challenges—in perspective.

"My mother was strict and demanding. My duty was to bring good grades home. My mother was most interested in making me independent and building my character. . . . She taught me that it all depended on me, so I took responsibility for myself very early on. My mother survived fourteen months in a concentration camp in her early twenties, so feeling sorry for myself was not an option. I am so grateful that my mother pressured me to build my character. She made me strong and independent, made me accept who I was, and made me want to do the best I could."

The Toll It Takes

But what happens when a girl can't handle all of the pressure that she is under to excel? The demands of school, wanting to please your parents, and the constant quest to be pretty and thin—all of these can really take a toll. Some of the girls in my task-force group shared with me how common eating disorders have become. Girls start to abuse their bodies in one way or another, and many develop an eating disorder. And what's so alarming is that many girls think this condition is actually cool.

All the girls I talked to knew at least one friend who was battling bulimia or anorexia, and many said that the pressure to be thin made them "anxious," and that they themselves had "tried to throw up" before. As Tara, age nineteen, explained to me, "There was a girl in my school who had an eating disorder and was super-skinny. My friends and I were really intrigued with the idea, and we would take tips from her. We wouldn't go to the extreme, but we used this problem to our advantage. It was fascinating." And Sarah, age fifteen, had this to say: "You need to drink supplement shakes because it's a craze to be skinny. You have to have bones and still be curvy."

It seems always to go back to the pressure they feel to be thin. Eighteen-year-old Laura said, "At my school there are a lot of girls with eating disorders. They get skinnier and

Girls Inc. Link: Top Five Worries

According to the Girls Inc. "Supergirl Dilemma" study, "The top five things that girls say they worry about are getting good grades in school, someone close to them getting sick or dying, how they look, their weight, and being made fun of or teased."*

*"The Supergirl Dilemma: Girls Grapple with Mounting Pressure of Expectations."

skinnier, where you can start to see their bones. I had a friend who, whenever she looked in the mirror, still thought she was fat. I told her that she was killing herself."

Not surprisingly, a few of the celebrities with whom I spoke had waged their own battles with eating disorders and they are hoping you can learn from their experiences.

KELLY CLARKSON ON THE PRESSURE TO BE THIN

Every time I've interviewed *American Idol* winner Kelly Clarkson, she has seemed very grounded despite all her fame. I love her fun spirit, her honesty, her drive, and of course her talent. When I told her I was writing this book, she felt it was so important to help girls overcome feelings of low self-esteem and wanted to share this story with you:

"Both girls and guys look at me and say, 'Oh, it's so easy for you,' but they don't know my story. Everyone has some kind of insecurity in their past, especially around junior high. Oh God, I remember during my freshman year in high school, and I was trying out for a musical. I knew I was better vocally (I could actually hit the notes) than two other girls who were auditioning, but the other two girls were tiny and beautiful, like pageant queens. I thought I was going to get the part because I was perfect for it—better acting, better singing. But I didn't get the part. The director and producer actually said to me, 'Oh, you didn't get it because you're too fat for the role.' At the time, I weighed a hundred and twenty pounds. I was like, 'What?' I had never thought I was too big, but when someone points that out to you, it sticks in your head, and you think, *Oh, there is something wrong with me and I need to fix it.*

"I didn't know how to fix it until I heard a girl at my school talking about [throwing up]. And I figured, *I can do that.* So for the next six months of my life, I was bulimic. I can't even describe how bad that felt; it's almost like anorexic people who look in the mirror and they see fat even though they weigh only ninety pounds. As absurd as it sounds or looks, you can't explain that reality to someone. It was only about six months of my life, and then I went cold turkey one day. Thank God. I realized that what I was doing was very destructive. I said to myself, 'This is not good.' I knew I had been miserable ever since that day [I was told I was too fat for the part]. Luckily, I had a good head on my shoulders, because most kids in those situations really suffer. Anorexia and bulimia are not easy things to get over. They are almost worse than a drug habit, because it's not like something in your system; it's actually your head and your mind. I think self-esteem always comes down to you and yourself. People take pictures of you and maybe it's not the most flattering picture, but you have to say to yourself, *I'm good, though, I don't really care, I'm cool, I'm healthy, I can run four miles, I'm cool.* I think at the end of the day it's how you feel about yourself, not what you look like or how much you weigh."

Before Kelly could get back on track, she had to face the reality that she was hurting herself. Her battle with bulimia clearly helped her prove to herself the strength of her own convictions. She came to believe that she was indeed talented—and look at the success she has achieved!

KATHARINE MCPHEE ON PROCESS

Singer Katharine McPhee, who also dealt with the intense pressure and incredibly rigorous schedule of competing on *American Idol,* has been very vocal about her own battle with an eating disorder when she was a teenager. She wants you to know that getting over any unhealthy behavior is a process.

"Fortunately, I had my mom, who really forced me at seventeen to deal with my problems with food. She supported me and helped me to take little steps to make it better. Now, did it get better? No, not immediately. It's a process. It's something that no one can force you to do. You have to really want to do it yourself. You need to be able to take responsibility for getting over whatever it is that you want to get over. I think the important thing is to find people in your life, whether it be your mom or your sister, your teacher, your high school counselor, somebody you can speak to if you are having issues. Because again, it's about taking responsibility and not about putting it on the back burner and then suddenly getting a drug addiction or sleeping around because you're trying to cope with this or that. And the earlier you deal with it and the more you get into helping yourself and finding a spiritual balance, the better off you're going to be in your twenties or thirties."

MEREDITH VIEIRA ON CRASH DIETS

Even someone as grounded as *Today* show host Meredith Vieira was not immune to the pressure to be thin growing up. She told me this story of how body image affected her as a young girl:

"It was the summer before I entered seventh grade. I was probably eleven years old, and pudgy. One day I was riding my bike around the neighborhood and a so-called friend yelled out, 'Hey, Fat Butt.' I was so devastated by that comment that I went on a crash diet, consuming nothing but basically Tab, apples, and Ritz crackers for a month. I lost a lot of weight that summer, but I didn't lose it out of self-esteem, I lost it out of shame. As it turns out, the girl who made the comment didn't even remember saying it when I brought it up to her in the fall. And that's when I realized that the biggest problem wasn't the comment itself; it was how I had perceived it. I let it define me. I've been working on my self-esteem ever since."

HEATHER MILLS ON KNOWING YOURSELF

Heather Mills has seen a lot of women with eating disorders in her life, but she says a strong sense of self helped her avoid the pitfalls: "I was a model for a long time, and they always used to say, 'You better lose five or six pounds.' And I'd say, 'That's not going to happen. You better choose another model—I like to eat.' That was just my personality. I didn't succumb to being told what to do. I know who I am."

DARA TORRES ON NOT KEEPING HER SECRET

Dara Torres. The name just conjures up strength and confidence. I first met the five-time Olympic swimmer, mother, and motivational speaker during the Beijing Olympics. Hoping to inspire girls to never abuse their bodies, she speaks candidly about her past struggle with bulimia and the role pressure played in her illness.

"I definitely think pressure was behind my eating disorder. I've learned there are other ways of dealing with pressure. The biggest one is going to talk with someone. Communication is so important. You need to try and find someone you are comfortable with so you can share your problems. I kept my eating disorder a secret for four years, but once I got down to why I developed it, I was able to start my recovery."

Party Like a Rock Star

Peer pressure and the role it plays in getting us to do things just to be accepted by the crowd—boy, do I know about that! In high school, I didn't like to drink. Not because I thought I was too young (although I was!), but because I just didn't like the taste of alcohol. I remember going to a party with a group of my friends, and it seemed like everyone was drinking. One of the kids poured me a drink, and just to be cool and go along with the crowd, I accepted it. I don't remember what was in that glass, but it was strong! Because I had such a low tolerance for alcohol, it went straight to my head. I started getting my groove on on the dance floor, a'swinging and a'swaying. I remember there being a big disco ball spinning above and a colorful strobe light (hey, it was the eighties!) reflecting off the ball. I kept looking at it, my head pounding, being mesmerized . . . and I started to get dizzy and sick. All of a sudden I ran off the dance floor, leaving the guy I was dancing with standing all by himself. I ran out the door and into the parking lot and fell down onto the ground. All I can say is, thank goodness there was no YouTube because someone would have had a video of a drunken fool. Not cute!

When I think about that moment, I realize the satisfaction of "fitting in" was so temporary, so fleeting. For an hour, I was having fun with the crowd by being "one of them," but shortly after, the party was over and I was sick. And I had indulged in something I didn't even enjoy. What would have happened if I had just said no? Maybe those kids wouldn't have hung out with me. Or maybe I would have had a good time anyway without putting myself in a precarious situation.

Now, as an adult, I have chosen not to drink. When I'm at a party or out to dinner with other adults, and people find out I don't drink, some will find it strange—as though there is something wrong with not wanting to drink. I've had some people try sooo hard to get me to have a cocktail with them even though I insist that I don't want one. They will look puzzled and ask, "Why not? Why don't you drink?" I usually politely say, "The same reason I don't eat okra. I don't like the taste."

I know from talking with girls across the country that many of you are feeling this same kind of pressure. As Stephanie, eighteen, said, "My friends are always trying to get me to smoke with them because they think it makes them look cool." And Sarah, fifteen, explained, "I definitely know that when I go to parties, people are going to make me do stuff."

Having the will and the strength to resist peer pressure to drink or smoke or starve yourself to be thinner gets that much harder when bad behavior is sometimes glorified in the media. Amy Winehouse sings about rehab, and then goes into it. Other young celebrities get checked in to facilities because their drinking or drug use has gotten out of control. Some women in magazines are so skinny that it seems obvious they have an eating disorder. Yet they are becoming famous through the coverage of their exploits! Something's warped in all that. In the end, we all know that more than likely what led these people to drink in excess or do drugs or not eat enough is pressure—not the pressure itself but how they were trying to manage that pressure. We should feel sorry for people with such problems, but we should also try to learn from their mistakes.

The girls I talked to told me directly: They want better role models who don't make drugs and drinking cool.

When celebrities go to rehab, TV makes it sound real cool. It's not a negative thing, but it should be. —TARA, NINETEEN

The media needs to realize that they have a big responsibility to focus more on positive than negative. Instead of glorifying rehab and drinking, there are more important things to focus on. —MARTY, EIGHTEEN

Michelle, seventeen, said it best: "I like celebrities who are original. The ones who are positive and tell us how to overcome some of the stressful things we are going through."

Your Health

For you as teenagers, it's so important that you look for healthy and positive ways to manage and cope with stress. Exercising, sports, writing in your journal, listening to positive, uplifting music, and creating art—these are all ways to chill, "veg out," and download your feelings. During times of confusion and intense feelings, the idea of sorting things out in your head might seem just too difficult, but simple activities can actually make you feel better. The endorphins from exercise and the calmness that comes from working out can teach your body to manage the stress hormones, so that you can control how you feel to some degree. Drugs, alcohol, and cigarettes are all temporary fixes that hurt you—now and in the future.

What I have gathered from the girls around the country, as well as certain celebrities who have won their own battles, is that those girls who were able to rely on their growing self-esteem and ability to listen to their own inner voice were able to defend against any pressure to do something they didn't want to do.

Take Care of Yourself

I have been blessed with a wonderful career. I get to meet some really interesting people whose work in television, film, and music I admire. I have been able to attend many exciting events and have traveled all around the world. I love what I do, but there are days when my schedule gets so hectic, I am just totally stressed out. I feel like I just don't know how I can manage another trip, another day spent packing my suitcase and fighting the airport crowds and just being away from home, my family, and my close friends.

So I decided to make managing the stress in my life a priority. I keep a prepacked bag with all my toiletries in it so that's one less thing for me to think about. I get to the airport early so I'm not running to the gate, feeling like a crazy person. I take inspirational books with me and relish the time in the air not having to listen to beeps on my BlackBerry. When I get to my destination, I'll book a massage at my hotel and work out in the gym before I leave for an assignment. All these tricks help make traveling less stressful, and I actually find myself looking forward to the trip! I've also learned to take a jam-packed week in small chunks. If I think about all I have to do at one time, I'll get overwhelmed. If I handle the week day by day, sometimes hour by hour, I find I can get through it much more easily.

This is what I do. Have you ever reflected on what you do to take care of yourself? Some of the celebrities and professional women shared with me some great advice.

Diane Sawyer on the Power of Laughter

Diane Sawyer is one of broadcast journalism's most prominent and successful figures. She's the anchor of both ABC's *Good Morning America* and *Primetime Live* as well as an award-winning investigative journalist. It's an understatement to say she has an incredibly busy schedule. What's her secret for maintaining her balancing act and staying positive?

"I think the saving thing is always laughter. Find the person who laughs at the thing [you] doubt in [your]self the most, and they will help you tame it. Express that doubt to a girlfriend. And help her laugh, too. Sometimes acting brave makes you brave. I know it."

Vanessa Williams on Taking Things Personally

Tony, Emmy, and Grammy nominee Vanessa Williams is a multitalented singer and actress who has achieved great success on television, in film, and onstage. She's also mom to four kids, three daughters and a son. She knows firsthand how media images can shape the way young ladies feel about themselves and offered some great advice on how to deal with the pressure that sometimes results from comparing ourselves with others and coming up short.

"One of the hardest things to practice every day as a young girl is *not* to take everything personally. It's actually one of the hardest lessons no matter what age you are. You never know what's going on with the person next to you, what just happened to the other person across from you, and what might be in store for that person who just gave you a dirty look. We, as women, internalize so many feelings and think we're often to blame for everyone's actions and reactions.

"So, next time someone rolls their eyes at you or says an unkind word about you, think about what *they* could be insecure about. What is it that you possess that they are angry that you have? I'm certainly not saying that you should be a doormat and allow others to walk all over you, but rather, take a breath before reacting to an unexpected comment, and have compassion. You'll feel better about yourself for not going there and feel sorry for the other person's bad behavior. In the end, you win."

GOVERNOR KATHLEEN SEBELIUS ON TEAMWORK

Kansas governor Kathleen Sebelius, who played various sports as a high school student, found that her experience being on a team helped to offset the everyday pressures of being a teenager.

"I think the whole notion of teamwork is important—whether it's a project getting done at work or surviving life with your family or playing a sport. Being on a team helps you learn how to use and maximize everybody's talent, how to share, how to become more unselfish—in other words, not everyone can always have the ball or be the one dribbling down the court or scoring all the points. Those life lessons about shared winning and shared losing often come initially out of sports activities. A lot of girls frankly just miss that piece of the puzzle, miss that ability to compete and take some risks."

JULIANNE MOORE ON THE POWER OF READING

Actress Julianne Moore found solace in reading.

"The one thing that always held a tremendous amount of meaning for me was reading. It was something I did for pleasure, and it helped me understand the world around me. Also, as a kid who moved constantly, it helped me feel less alone. Strangely, acting was then a natural progression—it was like being in the story. Once again, it gave me a tremendous sense of meaning, and therefore—*self-esteem*!"

Pressure. It can be good or bad, but either way it can take over our lives if we don't find ways to control and manage it. We all get caught up in the frenzy of trying to meet expectations, whether academic, social, or related to how we look. Pressure to be perfect can be brought on by our parents, our friends, our job, the media, or just our own imagination. Building our self-esteem means that we work hard but give ourselves downtime. We keep our social lives in perspective and don't take on too many obligations. We have to remember that when we are dealing with so much pressure, we shouldn't abuse our bodies or allow others to convince us to do things that we know are not right. We are much too smart and too important to let that happen!

Chapter Six

·········

You Are in Charge

SEX AND BOYS

Most parents would be surprised at the amount of pressure we are under to . . . have sex. If they really knew, they probably wouldn't let us out of the house.

— Bree, seventeen

Do you feel pressure to have sex?

The mood in the room started to shift when I asked this question to all the girls in my task-force meetings. There were sighs, giggles, then silence—each one looking around the room to see who dared tackle this topic first.

Sixteen-year old Caitlin was one of the first to speak up. "Yes, all the time. Some of my friends are like, 'Oh, it's so much fun, you should find some guy to do it with,' and I'm just like, 'No thank you.' I feel that sex should be with somebody special, not just some random guy that I'm dating for a month or something."

Theresa, who's only fifteen, said this: "Most of my

friends who have had sex before told me that they regretted it afterward. So why should I run out and do it?"

Eighteen-year-old Zoe was succinct: "I'm a virgin, but all of my friends are sexually active."

I have to say, I was really surprised to hear just how much pressure girls feel to have sex. It seems a lot of girls are having sex, even though they really don't feel they're ready. Many of them don't understand the dangers and that they are making choices that are jeopardizing their health and that chip away at their self-esteem.

As a young woman, you receive messages about sex on a daily basis, and what many of you are saying is that you feel confused about how to handle the pressure to do something that you don't feel emotionally ready to handle. You know that adults want you to wait before jumping into a physical relationship—you're clear about that. But what's confusing for many girls is when boys are putting pressure on you, saying things like, "You would if you loved me." And then there are the so-called girlfriends who tell you you'll feel so much more mature if you just go ahead and have sex. On top of that, you're confronted with sexual images all the time—when you turn on the television, open a magazine, log on to the Internet, go to the movies, or listen to the radio. You couldn't escape it if you tried!

After being in the television industry for many years, I've become more and more concerned about all of these sexual images bombarding you. My younger sister, Jewel, who is seventeen, told me that she and her friends will be singing along to a new song because they like the beat. It's only weeks later, when they stop to really listen to the lyrics, that they'll realize that the words they've been saying are so sexed up! So many of the songs are sexually explicit, violent, and degrading toward females. How can we help but take in those not-so-subtle messages?

Pressure Comes from All Sides

I think most of my friends who have had sex did it because their boyfriends begged them to. After a while, you're just like, "Well, if I don't, maybe some other girl would."   —ERICA, SIXTEEN

Boys do act like you're crazy if you don't want to have sex. They try to act like you're the only one not doing it. It's pretty pathetic.   —TAMMI, SEVENTEEN

The pressure to have sex is not only coming from boys, but the girls are joining in as well. A girl in one of my task-force groups told us that many girls think they instantly become more mature—more of a woman—after they have sex for the first time. Ironically, that is one of the most *immature* reasons to have sex.

As fifteen-year-old Kalie remarked, "Some girls, they just lay down with somebody and they don't really have any feelings for them. They are making really bad choices."

Ultimately, with bad choices comes regret—and very often lasting consequences.

"Most of the time, young girls are having sex and getting pregnant to keep the guy. And then he leaves you anyway and you grow up to be a single parent," Paige, eighteen, told me in disgust.

"The first time I had sex, I really regretted it. I wanted it to be special, but I chose the wrong guy to do it with. I thought he was my boyfriend, but then he started having sex with everyone in my school. Nobody will ever be special to him," Eva, age eighteen, shared with me sadly.

Laura, also eighteen, learned the consequences of an impulsive decision. "I have a nine-month-old daughter. When I first found out I was pregnant, I was shocked, angry, and disappointed. I was very naïve about protecting myself during sex."

Some girls I talked to were able to resist the pressure to have sex, while others were not. Many girls talked about giving in to the pressure to have sex because of their low self-esteem. On some level, they thought they were pretty and desirable if a boy wanted to have sex with them. I will never forget when one girl, Paula, eighteen, told me this very heartbreaking story before breaking down in tears: "I lost my virginity at thirteen. I felt I wasn't fully accepted by society. I didn't have long wavy hair. I had short locks. I met this guy and he validated my beauty. I didn't get it from home. He told me, 'Oh my God, you're so pretty.' Within two weeks I lost my virginity. You know, your mother or father, they can tell you, 'You're a beautiful girl.' "

KATHARINE McPHEE ON FEELING GOOD ENOUGH

What *American Idol* runner-up and recording artist Katharine McPhee told me is so true, and I wish all girls would understand the message: Having sex to feel good about yourself is a mistake that never has the intended result.

"Don't look for that reassurance that you are special from other people because you will never get it. A guy will never make you feel good enough. It comes from inside and whatever it is that you believe. For me, it only comes from an inner peace that you get from a higher power. No one is going to love you the way God will." .

QUEEN LATIFAH ON AVOIDING HURT

If you've made a mistake, or had sex but now no longer want to, you need to remember that there is always room to change; you *can* change your mind. When it comes to empowering girls to take control of their lives and make educated, informed decisions about their bodies, Queen Latifah is one of those celebrities who is truly committed to that cause.

> "Any time I did something that my gut told me was not right for me, I would feel punished—like in my initial love choices. I would decide to be with someone physically based on material things—what he wanted to give me and shower me with. I would ingratiate myself to him and then sleep with him. And then afterward, I felt disgusting—really gross and nasty. I felt dirty and I hated myself. And that feeling was so horrible to me that I decided I would never do that again."

JENNIFER LOVE HEWITT ON BEING READY

Like so many of the girls in my task-force groups, Jennifer remembered feeling not at all ready to be sexual. As she recalled:

> "One day you're going to realize that your gut instinct is worth so much. I would say to young girls, 'If you're not ready, you're not ready.' I was one of those very young girls who saw a lot of stuff going on and had friends who were doing stuff, and I was like, 'Oh

my gosh, what's wrong with me? Why am I not there yet? Why does my brain not work the way theirs do? What is it in me that is making me different?' I just realized that I was different. I wasn't ready. I didn't want to do that stuff. That's not where I was in my life, and that's okay.

"You have to be absolutely ready for sex. It's absolutely a serious thing when you're a teenager. There are a lot of consequences to go with it, and quite honestly, when you're a teenager, there are way too many other things going on. You've got too many hormones, too many questions, and you aren't really sure who you are. I would say wait. When you're ready, you'll be ready. No matter what, remember the entertainment industry is just there for fun. I think if young people, particularly, stopped making what they see in the media as [the source of a] rule book for what they are supposed to be doing, it would be a lot easier.

"If you're not ready, that just means you're not ready. It doesn't mean you're less than anyone else or not as smart or not as developed or whatever it is. In fact, I think people who stop and think about wise choices in their life, and who do things a little bit slower than normal because they want to be logical, ethical, and moral, and really think before they jump off the bridge, I think those are the smartest people."

The Media Doesn't Always Help

As Jennifer mentioned, the pressure to be sexual is reinforced by the media. As eighteen-year-old Raven said, "We can't escape it. Sex is everywhere! And if we have entertainment where the theme is always sex, kids are going to be more inclined to have sex, because they see it all the time. On all the TV shows that we watch . . . it's there."

And seventeen-year-old Ariel said, "Not everyone is

having sex. It just appears that way through the media. And sex is not something you should play around with. There are serious consequences if you are not careful."

Emma, fifteen, was aware of the power of the media to reinforce girls being sexual: "The media needs to send strong messages to young people—very strong—that sex is not all pleasure, it's not all fun and games, but there are serious consequences."

What really got girls talking in my task-force groups was the depiction of females in many music videos. As thirteen-year-old Megan said, "I don't blame the media for everything. However, some of these rap artists need to know that they make the sexual stuff they sing about sound really cool. A lot of kids, who are not really ready for sex, are saying, 'Hey, let's try that!' "

Sheila E. on the Video Scene

After Megan made that point, I called on my friend, world-famous percussionist Sheila E. She now counsels young people through her charity, the Elevate Hope Foundation, and has some very strong feelings on this topic.

"The video scene is pretty embarrassing. I have to say, I was there at one point and now that I'm older and I'm changed, I think, *What the* heck *was I doing?!* When I see these young girls today in these music videos, I don't want to call them video whores, but they're just wanting to be in the video to meet this rapper or artist, and they are pretty much naked, and a lot of them don't even get paid, just about. That image of being cool is not cool. It's heartbreaking to see these images being played on television right now."

JAMIE LEE CURTIS ON OBJECTIFICATION

. . . .

Golden Globe–winning actress and bestselling author Jamie Lee Curtis grew up in the entertainment business. She also has very strong feelings about how the media's images of young women can affect the way girls feel about themselves.

"The messages from the media and entertainment . . . that objectify and sexualize women are becoming epidemic and ubiquitous. How can a young woman today develop literally, physically, mentally, spiritually, sexually, and internally while being bombarded by these obscene messages and stereotypes every second?"

Do You Know the Dangers?

Recently Girls Inc., the organization I am involved with, sent me an email with a startling statistic: After a fifteen-year decline, teenage pregnancy is on the rise. I thought to myself, *How can this be true, with so much information out there on sex and health education?*

Part of the problem is that many girls don't have accurate information about sex and don't seem to understand the dangers—not only in terms of pregnancy (which can be a shortcut to dropping out of high school, being a single mother, and living in poverty) but also sexually transmitted diseases (STDs). Let's get real here, ladies. Did you know that you can get an infection from oral sex? Did you know that many guys don't even know they are carrying an STD and therefore don't realize they can infect a young woman? Did you know that many STDs can make it much harder—

and sometimes impossible—for you to have children? And that some STDs put you at a higher risk for cervical cancer? No boy is worth all that.

Sex Does Not Make the Woman

I've got to admit, when we were in high school, we hadn't heard of AIDS or many of the STDs that you are taught about today in health class. In my school of four thousand I don't remember one girl who got pregnant—it would have been the biggest scandal in the school! As I was writing this book, I thought a lot about the pressures we were under then, and they certainly don't compare with what you deal with today. But one thing was similar—the pressure from boys. I called a few of my old high school friends to ask what they remember from that time, and one of them reminded me of a story from when we were teenagers.

"When I was dating my first boyfriend, he kept pushing me to have sex. He kept telling me that since we loved each other, it was time to show how much we were committed physically. You know the first thing he said to me after we had sex for the first time? You're a *woman* now. Geez. And I was dumb enough to believe that *stupid* line!"

She and I had a good laugh about that moment. We laughed because we know now how completely ridiculous the notion of sex making the woman really is. Just to be clear, let me say it again: Having sex does *not* make you a woman. It is a much more mature decision to say, "I'm not ready. And if you don't respect that, I will find someone who will." And believe me, you will!

Girls Inc. Link: Fast Facts About Teenage Sex and STDs*

- Until a young woman is twenty-five, her cervix is more vulnerable to sexually transmitted diseases (STDs) because it's not fully developed.
- More than a third of young women ages fifteen to seventeen think oral sex is not as big a deal as intercourse.
- At least one in four teenage girls nationwide—more than three million teens—has a sexually transmitted disease, according to the first study of its kind in this age group.
- In a 2004 study conducted by the Centers for Disease Control, teens were tested for four infections: human papillomavirus, or HPV, which can cause cervical cancer and affected 18 percent of girls studied; chlamydia, which affected 4 percent; trichomoniasis, 2.5 percent; and herpes simplex virus, 2 percent.
- The rate of HPV, an STD that causes cervical cancer, has increased since 2004.

If you have any questions about sex, STDs, pregnancy, or other topics, please find a reliable source. Girlsinc.org offers a lot of information, as well as specific links to resources across the United States. You can also ask your doctor, who will keep information private and confidential. The point is, you have to take responsibility. It's up to you to get the information so you can make the wisest, most informed decision.

*Girls Inc., "Girls and HIV, AIDS, and STDs" (2007 fact sheet), www.girlsinc.org/downloads/GirlsandSTDs.pdf.

What You Seem to Want and Need

The girls I talked to around this country were asking for more direct talk from their parents or guardians; they wanted information about sex and about relationships so they can make their own informed choices. As Zoe, age eighteen, said, "I would love for my parents to be straight-forward with me. Don't beat around the bush. You know, tell me, 'When you have sex, this is what happens.' "

Another young girl, only thirteen, said this: "I have this friend [who's] thirteen and she's pregnant. She keeps saying that she wished her mom would not have been so closed up about telling her the dangers that come with sex."

Of course, it's not always easy for parents or girls to talk about sex. As Tracy said, "The sex talk is embarrassing. When my mom had it with me, I felt soooo uncomfortable. My mom didn't go about it the right way."

NANCY O'DELL ON QUESTIONING YOUR IDOLS
. . . .

Nancy O'Dell was insightful about keeping the media in perspective and staying close to your own values:

> "If [you] actually pay attention to what is going on in the media and don't just immediately follow what everyone is doing but instead *question* what they're doing, then you can actually learn from the mistakes of your favorite idols. Talk about *your* family's values and whether you believe the way the young TV/movie star is dressing and acting is right or wrong. Talk with your parents, siblings, and friends about what message the star is sending out and question why. And keep talking about what a positive role

model should be like, and try to find those stars who follow your same ideals."

If your parents aren't forthcoming with information about sex and relationships, and if you weren't listening in your sex-ed class at school, here's what I can tell you: Respecting your body is one of the most important things you

---

Girls Inc. Link: Avoid Risky Behavior

Girls Inc. works to motivate girls to avoid risky behavior and to make informed, responsible choices for their health, their families, and their futures. The organization believes that every girl deserves a chance to discover all she can be in life, and she deserves support from adults along the way. As part of its mission to inspire girls to be strong, smart, and bold, especially in terms of respecting their sexuality, Girls Inc. describes these three inalienable rights:

Truth: Girls have a right to accurate and timely information when they want it and in language they can understand.

Trust: Girls are entitled to support and respect from caring adults who believe girls can make good decisions.

Technology: Girls deserve the skills and resources to make good decisions and avoid early pregnancy (these resources include contraception, disease prevention, and general reproductive-health services) whether they are sexually active now or will be later in life.*

---

*www.girlsinc.org.

can do, and whether to have sex with someone or not is one of the most important decisions you can make. Remember that having sex will not do anything to keep a guy or get him to like you more. No matter how it appears on television, sex does not make you cool. Dressing like a video girl will get you one kind of guy—the guy that wants to sleep with you. That's it. Last but not least, remember that you only have to have sex once to get pregnant or to get a sexually transmitted disease. Either will change your life forever. Your health and your future are too important to risk them on something you're not 100 percent sure about. Listen to yourself and what your heart might be telling you. If you don't feel ready to have sex, don't let *anybody* tell you otherwise!

I could write an entire book about sex and the teenage girl. What I've tried to do in this limited space is to encourage you to ask questions and to take the time to really think about whether you want to have sex now. If you do, consider whether your decision has been at all coerced—by boys who you like, by girlfriends who think having sex makes you cool, or by some other form of pressure.

I will leave you with these thoughts: Treat your body like a temple. You are the golden statue in its center. You are the soul that keeps it alive. When you respect yourself, giving thought to all your decisions, you will pave the way to a life in which all will treat you with the respect that you deserve.

Chapter Seven

·········

You Are Part of Something Bigger

GIVE BACK AND TAKE RESPONSIBILITY

My business philosophy has always been threefold: (1) do great work; (2) treat people with respect; and (3) give back. That's it. I believe that if you do those things, you will be successful. —TRISHA WILSON, ARCHITECT

"We are the world."

You probably were not even born when Michael Jackson, Stevie Wonder, Cyndi Lauper, Tina Turner, Billy Joel, and many other artists recorded that famous song to raise money for famine relief in Africa and began a movement that inspired global awareness of how interconnected we all really are. But thanks to YouTube, that moment in history will live on forever. Whenever you watch the video, you might be like me and start swaying from side to side with your arm in the air, singing along with the collected stars. It feels good to give back, and that song motivates me to do so.

Many of the celebrities, athletes, and professional

women I spoke to for this book told me they have a pressing need to connect with their community and become part of something bigger. Self-esteem is rooted in knowing that you have a purpose—that because you are here, and decided to use your energy to lend a helping hand, someone else's life is a little better. When any of us shift the focus from ourselves—our problems, what's not right with our life, what we wish were different—and begin to concentrate on helping others, we automatically begin to see our glass as half-full instead of half-empty. Many of the girls in my task-force groups are just beginning to get involved in a way that makes them see how they, too, can make a difference. As sixteen-year-old Halli told me,

> "My dad made me and my sister help with a clothing drive at our church, and he had us take some of our clothes to give away. We picked some stuff we didn't like anymore because they were out of style. Then my dad made us choose a couple of things that we still liked. We were so mad! But then when we got down to the church and saw all the people who were really poor and didn't have anything at all, especially the little kids, we felt like we should have given them more."

My niece, Angelica, fifteen, shared this:

> "I think it's important to give your time to help people who may be less fortunate than you or maybe somebody who just needs an extra hand. I think doing charity work helps me by making me feel proud that I was able to help someone. I think it also teaches me to be able to make and keep com-

mitments. And also I think having done volunteer work will help me when it comes to [getting into] college."

So in this chapter, as you listen to why the women I interviewed got involved with their communities—either in their own town or city or in a more global way—maybe you will feel inspired to give back. Maybe that means being a role model for girls who are younger than you. Maybe that means giving your time to help at a local church fair. By giving back to your community or people in need, you can all assume responsibility for other human beings, animals, nature, and the planet at large. This *is* your world!

Give Back

I grew up in a family of caregivers who I saw countless times take care of sick and dying relatives and friends. Watching them show the love they had for another person was certainly a motivator. I have come to learn that when I stop focusing on myself and what I don't have and start genuinely trying to help others who are less fortunate, I instantly feel more thankful for those things that I do have. And once you are truly committed, you gain a deeper understanding of why we all need to give back—not just by writing a check (although that's important, too) but especially with your time.

I used to volunteer in a children's hospital in Texas; my job was to oversee the playroom, keeping it neat and making sure all the toys and games were working properly and had all their pieces. The children would come into the room with their little hospital gowns on, searching for something fun to play with. I would try to entice them with a doll or truck—most of them had never seen so many toys and would jump for joy at the many choices. There were many kids who were too sick to leave their beds, so I would pick a bunch of toys, load them onto my cart, and wheel them around to the rooms. I felt like the ice cream lady. I would announce myself—"Toys! Toys!"—and was so happy at how excited the kids were to see me.

Here's what I want you to know: There are kids with serious, life-threatening diseases—cancer, AIDS—who struggle with pain and intrusive procedures every day but who complain *less* than many of us do on a daily basis about insignificant, trivial things like not having the latest fashions. My mother always tells me: "No matter how bad you think your life is, there is always someone who would trade spots with you in a heartbeat."

DIANE SAWYER ON EMPATHY AND CONCERN FOR OTHERS

Diane Sawyer shared this with me about giving back: "Nothing gives confidence more than steeping yourself in someone else's life and need. As soon as you turn the introspective spotlight on someone else, you can feel the strength flood in."

JAMIE LEE CURTIS ON ESTIMABLE ACTS

Jamie Lee Curtis weighed in on how giving makes us feel better inside, a goodness that can spread like wildfire.

"Self-esteem is rooted in estimable acts. Anything you work hard on or for is a good foundation and will lead to a good feeling about yourself. Early success and too much praise dulls the senses to what should be merit-based and fought for. Helping others, being brave, facing fears and limits and pushing past them is the way into a wonderful feeling of accomplishment and then into self-esteem."

Giving back takes so many forms: spending time with sick children, reading to a senior in a nursing home, counseling girls who don't have role models at home, planting trees, building homes, rescuing abused animals, even getting involved in politics. As sixteen-year-old Lyric told me, "Volunteering with a political campaign was an amazing experience for me. It's so important for young people to get involved. Even though we can't vote, we still have a voice, and it's our future we're handling."

JENNIFER LOVE HEWITT ON MAKING THE PLANET A BETTER PLACE

"When you're helping other people, it raises your self-esteem because you realize that you're being part of the world you're born into. We're all here to do the same thing. No matter what the circumstances, no matter what lifestyle, no matter what you look like, where you're from, how you got here, we are all human beings born to do the same thing; we're all here to be the best people that we can be and live a happy, healthy, existence on this planet. You realize when you help other people, you are truly doing what you're supposed to do—serve. You are respecting the gifts that you were given on this earth because you put in the time for humanity."

Be a Role Model

Whether we realize it or not, we are all role models. Lots of girls see me on TV and say they look up to me for guidance on how to have a career in broadcasting. I get many emails from girls telling me that they listen to how I speak, watch how I stand, and pay attention to how I hold the microphone. It's clear that they are trying to learn from how I interview people. But what really touches me most are the emails from girls who tell me how they have been inspired to help others because of the volunteer work that I do, especially with Girls Inc.

But being a role model doesn't mean you have to be in a position of authority. You can be a role model if you take the time to nurture confidence in younger people. You're learning how to use your own unique qualities to break glass ceilings and set your own rules about what is important. You never know who is watching you and learning by your example. You are somebody's role model today!

SPEAKER NANCY PELOSI ON HER ROLE MODEL

As a young girl growing up, Nancy Pelosi watched her mother's commitment to giving back to her community and clearly followed in her footsteps, taking on even more responsibility and becoming a role model herself to so many girls who aspire to become involved in public service.

"My mother showed me that more was possible for women. When I was growing up, my father served as the mayor of Baltimore with my mother at his side. She ran his campaigns out of our home and kept a close watch on constituent services. As first lady of Baltimore, she actively used her platform to improve housing in the city. My mother taught me the responsibility we all have to help those in need and showed me what a significant role women could play in politics as she worked hand in hand with my father to serve the people of Baltimore."

General Velma Richardson on Showing Up

Sometimes giving back means being a role model for others who need you. Once Retired General Velma Richardson rose through the ranks, an important part of her job was helping to shepherd other young women officers. And that meant for the long haul. As she said:

"They call themselves my babies, and I have been at every one of their changes in commands. It is important to be present and for them to know that you still feel connected to what is happening in their military lives and careers. Showing up is important."

Gina Davis on Becoming Part of the System

FBI agent Gina Davis shares that same mission to help other women who want to walk in her footsteps by helping to change the system:

"I felt it was my responsibility being part of the system to try to make it better for everyone else I encountered. I was trying to change all these misconceptions about law enforcement in the black community and all the communities of color. The only way to make it any better is for people like me and other folks to become part of the system. You can't change the system from the outside."

Julie Chen on Contagious Behavior

"Those who can relate to you will love [watching what you are doing] . . . while others fascinated by it will want to learn more by gravitating to you. Teach others what makes you good and different. Don't be afraid to take risks, and encourage others to do the same. Behavior is contagious . . . both good and bad. Be with those who support you, and support those you love. What goes around comes around."

How Can You Give Back?

When you first start thinking about how you can give back to your community, it can feel overwhelming—there are so many causes that need help, and it's hard to choose where to start! I always think it's best to begin with where your heart is. You want to do something authentically, and this happens when you truly care.

So let me ask you some questions and give you some ideas.

Do you like being with young children? Maybe you want to help out in your neighborhood by offering to do some babysitting.

If you like to read, you might find a local literacy organization that is looking for volunteers to read to young kids. So many classrooms are understaffed.

Are you comfortable in a hospital setting or spending time with senior citizens, who may not have any family? Maybe you'd enjoy volunteering at a hospital?

If you prefer to be more behind the scenes, maybe you could make phone calls for an organization in need of raising money. There are so many great advocacy programs in the areas of animal rescue, blood banks, cancer research, early-childhood intervention, global warming, pollution, and other causes.

Do you like animals? Maybe you want to volunteer at a pet adoption center, helping to take care of animals rescued from the street or abusive homes.

If there is a Big Brothers/Big Sisters organization in your area, maybe you could volunteer to be a big sister.

You don't have to run out the door right now. It takes time to figure out the best way to make a difference in the lives of others or make a positive impact on our environment. For more information, contact girlsinc.org, where you will find links to volunteer opportunities around the country.

I'll end this chapter with one more thought, from Joss Stone: "You have to be proud of who you are and keep doing what you like to do. Make yourself happy. Because if you're happy, the people around you will be happy."

In other words, what goes around comes around. We are all connected.

Chapter Eight

You Are You

REMAIN TRUE TO YOURSELF

*True self-esteem is realizing that you are valuable because
you were born. No matter where you come from, what color
your skin is, what people say about your family or what
mean things people may have done to you, because you were
born, you are important and you matter.*

— OPRAH WINFREY

Remaining true to yourself is a lifelong journey, and you
will grow and change and have to reassess how to be true to
yourself throughout your life. The best way to keep growing as a person is to challenge yourself to do things that you
never thought you could do. For me, writing this book was
that kind of challenge. I've spent so many years thinking
about how I could give back and make a contribution to all
the girls out there who struggle with self-esteem. I've always wanted to help girls see and feel the beauty inside of
them.

As with any important project or goal, I often second-
guessed myself, floundered, and even felt frightened putting
myself out there. But by focusing on what I wanted to say to

you all, I kept moving forward. I started small and compiled my thoughts, taking it one day at a time, and it's paid off. I've reached my dream of being a published author!

For all of you at the beginning of your lives, I want you to have big dreams, deep confidence, and an unshakable trust in your own self-worth. You can do anything if you set your mind to it.

Life Is a Process

When I listen to these powerful and influential women speak about their lives, I realize that those who feel most confident, who know how to recover their center when they slip or fall, are those who always remind themselves that life is a process. In other words, we all make mistakes—the key is to learn from these mistakes. There will be plenty of time and opportunity to do things differently in the future, but when you take a moment of reflection and ask yourself, "What can I learn from this experience?" not only will you be less likely to make another less-than-good decision, but you'll have grown—as a person, in confidence, and in strength. You take responsibility for your life—the good and the bad.

I hope that after reading this book you know that you've also got to treat yourself with kindness, compassion, and respect. When you listen to your gut and become aware of those times when you are comfortable and, more important, when you're not, you're actually learning about yourself and how to develop self-esteem. As so many of these celebrities and professional women have been saying, it's when you can truly listen to your inner voice that you will gain that trust in yourself and go for it.

Diane Sawyer on Turning It Around

....

This book has been all about self-esteem—how to get it, how to keep it. Diane Sawyer puts an interesting spin on how our self-doubts might actually be a great strength. "I've often wondered if shaky self-esteem isn't the companion of the intuition, sensitivity, and compassion we love in so many women. It helps us feel and not just think. And this is a powerful thing."

Helen Mirren on Being Fearless

....

Talented, sophisticated, Oscar-winning actress Helen Mirren has never been one to hold back when it comes to expressing herself. While I don't usually advocate profanity, I think Helen's advice here has a certain empowering ring to it.

"I think the best words that I can offer are ones that I do wish I had been taught to say, fearlessly and vehemently, and they are 'Why don't you just f__ off.' I often say this to myself when I open one of those 'Why don't you look like this?' or 'You're not as famous as this' articles in a magazine. However, when I am confronted by an energy or a commitment to life that I truly admire, I try to be inspired by that energy and that commitment. I try to learn from the positive and ignore the negative."

Queen Latifah on Being Patient

....

Queen Latifah knows a lot about the virtues of patience when it comes to growth:

"Be patient with yourself. I know it's hard—everything is so intense when you're young. Things are happening for the first time, and it feels like it's going to be the end of the world. But it's really not—you will survive, you just have to be patient. Be smart about things. I had no idea at fifteen that I would be an Oscar-nominated, Grammy-winning, Emmy-nominated entrepreneur, et cetera. I never knew those things would happen. Luckily, I made decisions that led me to those things—one of the biggest was the choice I made to love myself and be strong. Even if no one else loved me, I had to love me because there are times when you don't have a crowd to roll with. You have to stand on your own two. And you have to believe in yourself when no one else will. That's the only way you will accomplish your goals. Sometimes people just don't get it, but you get it. You have the dream; they don't have the dream. You have the vision; they don't have the vision. As long as you feel it and you believe in yourself and love yourself enough to make the right decision for yourself and surround yourself with people who are positive and don't want to tear you down every time you come up with an idea, you will move in that direction."

Governor Kathleen Sebelius on What Can Be Done

"I have a little leather plaque that sits on my desk that says, IT CAN BE DONE. For me, this is a very helpful saying, and I like to think that you start with the answer 'yes,' then you figure out what the questions are. Not 'Can you do this?' but 'Absolutely it can be done, you can do it.' Then ask yourself, 'What are the resources and helpers and opportunities that need to be created in order to accomplish this goal?'

"I think starting with an attitude of success makes all the difference in the world. That was drilled into me by my parents, who said it over and over again. I'm one of the fortunate ones who grew up with both a mother and father who basically said, 'Anything you want to do, you can do.' When people around me have been doubters at times, I have found it helpful just to get new friends, or find a new mentor, or go to someone else who doesn't have a limited view of what women can do."

India.Arie on Letting Your Pride Carry You

One woman who has never limited herself is artist India.Arie. I think she is one of the most unique and inspiring singers on the scene today. If you listen to the messages in her songs, you know that she wants all girls to feel comfortable in their own skin.

"Girls still struggle because no matter what anybody says, what matters most is what you think of yourself. It is something that has to come from the inside. I wrote about this in a song called 'Get It Together.' Because women have been marginalized and mistreated and objectified for thousands of years, it might take one step at a time, but the fact that there is movement at all is a powerful statement about where we are headed as a human race with respect to these issues.

"I want to tell girls out there to do the best you can to love yourself, but don't beat up on yourself when you start feeling down about gaining a little weight or your skin breaking out. It is okay to feel everything you feel, one step at a time, and the generation that follows you can build on your foundation. The key is to do the best you can in that moment. The more I learn, the more I realize that there is so much power in expressing *who I am,* and being the best at being *me*. There is only one you, and only you can develop that. Find pride in that, and let that pride carry you.

Listening to Your Inner Voice

We've all heard this advice before: Listen to your own voice. Pay attention to your gut. What do these phrases mean exactly? In the case of peer pressure (which we have talked about a lot in this book), even though you might have a desire to go along with the crowd, there is probably a little voice that tells you what everyone else is doing might just be against your own morals. Your inner voice always speaks to you, but it's often drowned out by the voice of fear that tells you you won't be popular if you don't do such-and-such.

The challenge is to quell that negative voice of self-doubt and replace it with positive messages like "I'll feel better about myself if I stick to my own values," and "I will find friends who appreciate me for who I am."

Virginia Madsen on the Truth of Your Inner Voice

Virginia Madsen has some more advice to help you embrace the real person deep inside you.

"I would say two things: that you must listen to your inner voice; it will tell you the truth. And you must find spiritual strength. That was something that really, really got me through. You know what's right and wrong. And you also know that you're not as bad as someone is telling you you are. Our inner voice will tell us the

truth. Listening to your inner voice helps you to know who you
really are, because that's who you are going to become."

LAILA ALI ON LISTENING TO YOURSELF

Laila Ali also spoke about how she relies on her inner voice to guide her.

> "I try to wake up and appreciate that I woke up. I try to start
> the day by wanting it to be a good day, a productive day. For me, lis-
> tening to my own intuition helps me avoid making mistakes. If I
> constantly think about whether or not I should or shouldn't do this,
> and I just go ahead and do it, then I always end up wishing I had
> just listened to myself. We all have an inner voice, and a lot of times
> we don't listen to it."

GARCELLE BEAUVAIS-NILON ON FOCUSING ON THE INSIDE

> "I just think that we just need to focus on the inside. At the end of
> the day, if it's your last day on earth, what are you most proud of?
> Who you are as a person, or what you look like? I mean, is it about
> having a hit movie, or having a great family?"

Becoming Who You Are Meant to Be

So much of what I have learned from the women I interviewed was about how to embrace yourself—warts and all.
They all knew that the less time and energy they gave to
worrying about what other people think, or comparing
themselves with others, the more their self-esteem grew.

I remember all the time I spent in high school trying to

Who Are You?

Whenever I feel pushed around by life and lose my center, I often ask myself some simple questions to remind myself of who I am. The next time you feel this way, or any way for that matter, ask yourself some questions that will help you remember the real you.

- How do I feel right now?
- What am I thinking about?
- How am I feeling about my body?
- Am I comfortable with my friends at school?
- Am I having trouble talking to someone about a difficult topic?
- What am I good at?
- What tasks or classes are more difficult for me?
- Am I getting enough rest and exercise?
- Am I paying attention to how I eat?

impress the wrong people, worrying about a boy who didn't like me, wishing that I looked different, and generally not accepting myself for who I was. I have a handful of friends from high school who I am still close to and talk to all the time, but trust me when I say that you will never see most of the people from high school again—except maybe at your class reunion. Years from now, it won't matter what the popular kids thought of you. You will one day laugh about the guy who dumped you. And you will be able to see clearly that what the media says is perfect is pure fantasy and most women don't (and shouldn't) look that way.

What *will* matter years from now is that you have

dreamed big and believed that anything is possible for you. Start doing that today, and for the rest of your life!

TICHINA ARNOLD ON CONCENTRATING ON YOU

A friend of mine, the actress Tichina Arnold, has enjoyed much success on television throughout the years. She has played many comedic roles that match her bubbly personality and love of life. Here is some great advice from Tichina for embracing the wonderful girl inside you:

> "Stop looking at and judging other people and pay attention to yourself. It's a great thing when you can look at what someone else is doing and be encouraged and motivated to enhance your abilities, but when you start to envy or emulate others, you are almost guaranteed to lose yourself. Concentrate on you and your strengths—nobody can be you and is capable of doing what you do."

And more of our celebrated women echoed the same advice:

CANDACE PARKER ON EXPRESSING YOURSELF

> "Basketball is basically an expression of myself, and I don't have to be anyone else on the court."

NANCY O'DELL ON BEING TRUE TO YOURSELF

> "Honoring your own values will only make you stronger and more liked and respected. Too often, young people think that giving in to peer pressure or doing what everyone else *says* they are doing will

make them more popular. Actually, the opposite is true. People who give in to things are weak and others will realize it and think less of them. You should be good to your bodies, too. Exercising and eating right to be healthy, not to be scary skinny, is important. And last, express the real person you are, and be proud of your individuality."

ALICIA KEYS ON YOUR SPECIAL SECRET

"Girls, I know how you feel. You are not strange for feeling self-doubt. Everyone does. Even the people who you think have it perfect or have it all. There's no such thing.

"Instead, find something special about yourself. Do you draw well? Maybe you're really smart and think of things in a more interesting way than your friends do. Learn how to play up the best parts of yourself and embrace those things. It can become your own special secret, and when you love something about yourself it really shines through naturally. Know that you are special and those who don't see how special you are don't deserve to know you. Remove negative people from your life. You don't need them. Once you get rid of people who try and tear you down, you can find the best parts of yourself. And every day, look in the mirror and say, "My heart is beautiful, I am special, and anything I can imagine and dream will be real in my life!" I promise you this works—I do it all the time!"

JULIE CHEN ON BEING TRUE TO YOURSELF

"There will always be someone out there who is prettier, skinnier, has more money or whatever, so forget trying to measure up to what they have. Instead, build yourself up based on what God gave you. We all have our own unique talents. It's what makes us all special. And what you have, someone else doesn't. That's why we're all individuals. We come with our own personality, style, sense of humor, looks, laugh, voice, and talent. Be true to yourself, be honest with yourself and others, and let your spirit come through."

LISA RINNA ON FOLLOWING YOUR PASSIONS

"The business I'm in is hard and challenging, but I love every minute of it because this is my passion! You have to always follow your passion in life, whatever it may be, and if you have more than one, which I know you do, then listen to your heart and go for all of them!"

SPEAKER NANCY PELOSI ON WHAT'S POSSIBLE

"I understand the difficulties and challenges young girls face growing up today. To all of you young girls who are not yet confident in your abilities and talents, I say, you may not realize it now, but you have the power to make your dreams a reality. Never give up. Anything is possible. If you remain focused on achieving your goal, you will succeed and realize your full potential."

So there you have it. I'm smiling and crying at the same time as I write these last lines to you. I want so badly for you to realize the potential that you have inside. I've gathered this wonderful collection of women with experience—who have been through every single thing you are going through now and will go through in the future—all to help you navigate these exciting and scary years with a little more help and guidance. I heard a tremendously moving gospel song this past weekend by Marvin Winans with the lyrics "A million didn't make it, but I was one of the ones who did." So many girls out there, for various reasons, will never see their light shine as brightly as it could. But *you* will be different. You will wake up every morning and give thanks for another day to be magnificent. You will *dream big* and carve a path for many other girls to follow their dreams. I believe that is your destiny!

Peace,
Shaun

More Information
on Girls Inc.

Girls Inc. is a national nonprofit youth organization dedicated to inspiring all girls to be strong, smart, and bold. With roots dating to 1864, Girls Inc. has provided vital educational programs to millions of American girls, particularly those in high-risk, underserved areas. Today, its innovative programs help girls confront subtle societal messages about their value and potential, and prepare them to lead successful, independent, and fulfilling lives.

Girls Inc. offers many resources for information on sexuality, violence, substance abuse, and other topics; tips for girls as well as their parents; and instructions on how to join or form a Girls Inc. group in your area.

Girls Inc.
120 Wall Street
New York, NY 10005-3902
tel: 212-509-2000
fax: 212-509-8708
website: www.girlsinc.org
email: communications@girlsinc.org

Emmy Award–winning journalist SHAUN ROBINSON is the weekend co-host of *Access Hollywood*. She has covered the red carpet for the Academy Awards, Golden Globes, Emmys, and Grammys. Her live coverage of "A Grand Night in Harlem" for the Black Sports and Entertainment Hall of Fame garnered her an Emmy Award. She has been a guest co-host on *The View* and has contributed reports to MSNBC, CNN, and *Today*. Robinson's many television and film credits include *Bruce Almighty*, *America's Sweethearts*, and *Everybody Hates Chris*. Robinson is on the national board of directors for Girls Inc. She also devotes her time to the Los Angeles County "Share Your Heart, Share Your Home" program, which helps find permanent homes for minority children waiting for adoption. A native of Detroit, Michigan, and a graduate of Spelman College in Atlanta, Shaun Robinson lives in Los Angeles.

For more information, and to continue the conversation about self-esteem and confidence with Shaun, visit her at www.shaunrobinson.com.

ABOUT THE TYPE

The text of this book was set in Janson, a misnamed typeface designed in about 1690 by Nicholas Kis, a Hungarian in Amsterdam. In 1919 the matrices became the property of the Stempel Foundry in Frankfurt. It is an old-style book face of excellent clarity and sharpness. Janson serifs are concave and splayed; the contrast between thick and thin strokes is marked.